A HISTORY OF CHESHIRE

Little Moreton Hall.
A beautiful example of a moated manor house. Most of the half-timbered building as seen today dates from about 1559 to 1589.

A HISTORY OF CHESHIRE

WITH MAPS AND PICTURES

by

DOROTHY SYLVESTER

(Formerly Reader in Geography in the University of Manchester)

Maps compiled by the author and drawn by

GEOFFREY BARBER

DARWEN FINLAYSON HENLEY-ON-THAMES

First published 1971

Copyright © 1971   *Dorothy Sylvester*

ISBN 0 85208 067 0

DARWEN FINLAYSON LIMITED
50A BELL STREET, HENLEY-ON-THAMES, OXON
PRINTED OFFSET LITHO BY BALDING & MANSELL LTD.
OF LONDON AND WISBECH

CONTENTS

MAPS

LIST OF ILLUSTRATIONS

The photograph of Beeston Castle, 1, is by Donald C. Good, whose copyright it is and by whose courtesy it is reproduced. The photograph of Sandbach Crosses, 3, is by Robert Newstead; those numbered 6, 9 and 11 of the churches are by Fred H. Crossley. All these and the two prints of Chester, 4 and 5, have been kindly lent, and are here reproduced by courtesy of the Rev. Canon M. H. Ridgway. The Diorama of Roman Chester, 2, is reproduced by courtesy of the Grosvenor Museum, Chester (copyright). The photograph of Nantwich Parish Church from Welsh Row, 10, is by C. V. Kendall and reproduced with his permission. The frontispiece and the photographs numbered 7, 8, 12 and 15 are copyright and reproduced by permission of Picturepoint Ltd. The photograph of Crewe Hall, 13, is by John Macdonald and the copyright of Calmic Ltd., by whose courtesy it is reproduced here. The photograph of Anderton Lift, 14, is the copyright of British Waterways and reproduced here by their courtesy. The two old prints of Stockport, 16 and 17 are reproduced by courtesy of Stockport County Borough Council and the blocks have been kindly lent by Messrs. McMillan Graham Publishers Ltd. The print of Congleton, 18, appears in *History of Congleton* ed. W. B. Stephens (1970) published by the Manchester University Press and is here reproduced by kind permission of the editor of the Congleton Chronicle. The photograph of Subsidence in Northwich, 19, is here reproduced by courtesy of Northwich Urban District Council; that of Port Sunlight, 21, by courtesy of UML Ltd. (copyright); and that of Stanlow Refinery, 24, by courtesy of Shell U.K. Ltd. (copyright). The aerial photographs of Birkenhead, Runcorn and Crewe, 20, 22 and 23, are the copyright of Aerofilms Ltd.

PREFACE

Cheshire has a long, proud, and unique history as a county palatine which only became part of the English Realm when, in 1536, the unity of England and Wales was achieved and the Marcher Lordships ceased to exist as such. Much splendid work has been published on various aspects and periods of the history and historical geography of the county and its parts both in papers and books, and the massive three-volume *History of the County Palatine and City of Chester* by George Ormerod, revised by Thomas Helsby in 1882 remains the standard work. At the other end of the scale one or two shorter histories of the county have been written, but all are now out of print. Indeed, my own interest in local history was first aroused when, at eleven, Oswald Estry's *History of Cheshire* was one of my school text books. But neither history nor its interpretation stands still, nor can the majority of the reading public, now deeply interested in the evolution of their own and other parts of Britain, get access to the weightier volumes, or find time to read them if they could. Many have therefore welcomed this series which the publisher and authors have designed to set forth the entire conspectus of the story of the counties from early times to the living present. Their brevity and conciseness, illuminated by maps and pictures offer, I believe, much to justify the inevitable omissions, but even these may, one hopes, be the very means of stimulating further study in the field and in the library. Meantime, the pace of change quickens, and the remarkable transformations which have taken place in the Cheshire scene since Ormerod and Helsby were writing is sufficient justification for unrolling the moving film of Time to the present day.

I should like to thank the following for their invaluable help, in reading the text, commenting on it, and making constructive suggestions: Mr. David Cleland, Mr. T. G. Dentith, Mr. D. F. Petch, the Rev. Canon M. H. Ridgway, Mr. & Mrs. J. H. Timmis, Mr. John Turner, and Mr. G. D. Twigg. In addition, useful information has been supplied by Mrs. Laura Carter, Mr T. G. Dentith, Mr J. Healey of Shell U.K. Ltd., Mr. M. C. Moore of UML Ltd., Mr. S. D. Lee of Calmic Ltd., Mr G. D. Twigg of B.P. Chemicals Ltd. (Murgatroyd's Division), and in addition I am grateful to Mr. F. A. J. Utting for his help in proof reading. The Clerks of many Cheshire Boroughs and Urban District Councils have sent information and Official Guides, and I trust that they will forgive me if I express my thanks inclusively. Not least, I should wish to acknowledge the unfailing help of Mr. Geoffrey Nulty, Editor of the *Winsford Guardian* who, from the time when he was my Assistant Editor in the production of *The Historical Atlas of Cheshire*, has always responded so willingly to my cries for aid. To Mr. Geoffrey Barber, senior technician in the Department of Geography, University of Keele, I am indebted for his admirable re-drawing of the maps which I compiled and designed for this volume.

D.S.

Wistaston 1970

I

The Shape of Cheshire

For four hundred years the extent of Cheshire has been very much as we know it today, but the Cheshire of which the shape is now so familiar and which has been compared with a teapot, is only the shrunken remnant of a once vast county.

The first written proof of its existence as a shire is to be found in the Alfredian Chronicle, compiled about A.D. 980, when it was called Legaceaster, 'the shire of the city of the [Roman] legions', or the shire centred on Chester. It had probably been shired or sheared from Mercia, the great Midland kingdom, a century earlier and was centred, like most of the shires, on a county town conveniently placed for its administration. The Anglo-Saxon shire almost certainly stretched westward as far as Offa's Dyke.

Cheshire reached its greatest extent during the early Middle Ages. In 1071, the Norman Hugh d'Avranches, nicknamed Hugh the Fat, was made Earl of Chester and in 1086, when the Domesday Book was compiled, the county of Chester (as it had then been named) was of major importance in relation to the March of Wales. It ballooned north to the river Ribble, including all south Lancashire and parts of the upper Yorkshire dales, west to the Clwyd over what was later to become Flintshire, and in the south-west it spread across the Dee over Welsh and English Maelor—land which later became eastern Denbighshire and the detached part of Flintshire between Shropshire and Cheshire.

In 1237, the earldom passed to the Crown and it has remained a royal earldom ever since. It was probably at that date that this, the largest of the marcher earldoms, became palatinate, that is an all-but independent territory where the King's writ did not run, a palatine county which could make its own

laws, administer its own courts and impose taxes. It retained these powers in full until 1536, and still retains the name with largely nominal meaning.

Lancashire, like Cheshire, had been a separate shire in the Anglo-Saxon period. It is thought to have regained its status as a county stretching south to the Mersey in the twelfth century, and in 1351 palatine status was conferred on the fourth Earl of Lancaster who was at the same time made a duke. The loss of south Lancashire was the second major cut in the size of the Norman county of Chester.

In 1284, when the treaty of Rhuddlan was drawn up at the conclusion of Edward I's successful campaigns in Wales, the first Welsh counties were created. Only one of these was in east Wales—Flintshire—and its formation brought Cheshire's western boundary eastward to the lower Dee and shifted it to the northern edge of Maelor Saesneg. At the same time, what is now Denbighshire was divided into four marcher lordships. These were only converted to shire ground in 1536, but eastern Denbighshire was lost to Cheshire at the same time as Flintshire.

From 1284 to 1536, Cheshire remained a palatinate under its royal earls and continued semi-regal in status, but its size was much as it is now, with Chester a bare mile from the county boundary. In 1536, by the Act of Union which brought all Wales and England under the English Crown, Cheshire at last became part of the English realm and sent its first members to the parliament at Westminster.

From that time onwards, changes in shape have been confined to minor adjustments of the boundary with other counties, for example, in the cession of the Wythenshawe area to Lancashire, the adjustment of the boundary to run along the Manchester Ship Canal between Runcorn and Partington in 1933, and the straightening of the boundary with Derbyshire in the Taxal area three years later.

I.   COUNTY AND DIOCESE

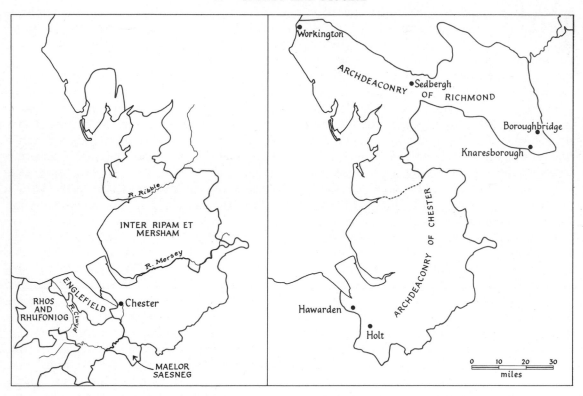

a. The county in Norman times stretched north to the River Ribble and on the south and west included what is now Flintshire and eastern Denbighshire. Conquest from time to time took the earls of Chester west of the Clwyd.

b. The Tudor diocese of Chester consisted of the two archdeaconries of Chester and Richmond, but by the twentieth century the formation of new dioceses north of the River Mersey and the cession of Welsh parishes to St. Asaph reduced it to almost the exact area of the present county.

II

The Geographical Setting

Cheshire is formed geologically like a shallow dish divided near the middle by a sharp, narrow ridge, flanked by a steep eastern edge and broken on the north where the Mersey valley lies across what structurally is still part of the same depression. This same syncline, along the Wilmslow-Prees axis, also extends into north Shropshire, but the last glaciation dumped hummocky moraine across it from east to west and the Cheshire-Shropshire boundary follows it. It is only a low rise but it helped to separate the streams draining to the Mersey and the Weaver from those flowing south to the Severn and it has constituted a minor but effective barrier between the two parts of the lowland and throughout later human history.

The Cheshire plain is underlain by Triassic rocks. Various sandstones predominate from the Central Ridge westwards, emerging from place to place and providing well-drained water-bearing sites especially favourable for early settlements. To the east, the deeper part of the syncline is infilled by Keuper Marls which are believed to have been exploited from Roman times for their important salt deposits. The entire plain has been glaciated and the deposits of boulder clay and sand, giving a gently rolling surface, cover most of the underlying rocks. Where clays predominate, as they do in the eastern basin, the natural vegetation is damp oakwood, difficult to penetrate and to clear and, as a result, this area was settled thinly throughout much of its history. In turn, it is flanked by the western bastions of the Pennines where the low Triassic sandstones of the Mow Cop—Congleton Ridge line herald the higher, gaunt uplands of the Millstone Grits, or the rather softer sandstones of the Coal Measures in the middle and northern parts of the Cheshire Pennines. The coal began to be worked in north-east Cheshire in the eighteenth century but its economic importance has been very minor compared with the coalfields of its neighbours Lancashire and Staffordshire. Although, like the Central Ridge, these relatively bare uplands were of significance in the prehistoric period, their later settlement history was confined largely to scattered hill farming and quarrying groups until the Industrial Revolution brought urban growth to the northern parts, but the springlines at their foot have long been the sites of villages and hamlets.

After the downhill movement of population in the Early Iron Age and the Romano-British phase, the broad valleys of the plain offered a greater attraction to settlers on account of their many economic advantages. Deep drift soils, fertile alluvium in the valley bottoms, comparatively level land and an assured water supply from streams and shallow wells in the alluvium and the glacial sands, timber for building and fencing, clay for brick making and many minor resources made them suitable for agriculturalists once the techniques of clearing and farming the deeply wooded lands were mastered. Their colonization, begun in the Early Iron Age and on a minor scale even earlier, advanced through the Dark Ages and by the late eleventh century the population of the west Cheshire valleys and of the Weaver belt was greater than in any other part of Cheshire except Wirral. Timber, cattle and corn brought widespread if modest wealth to these broad, river-drained lowlands. Only along the middle Mersey did extensive marsh delay settlement of a major valley.

The navigability of the more suitable

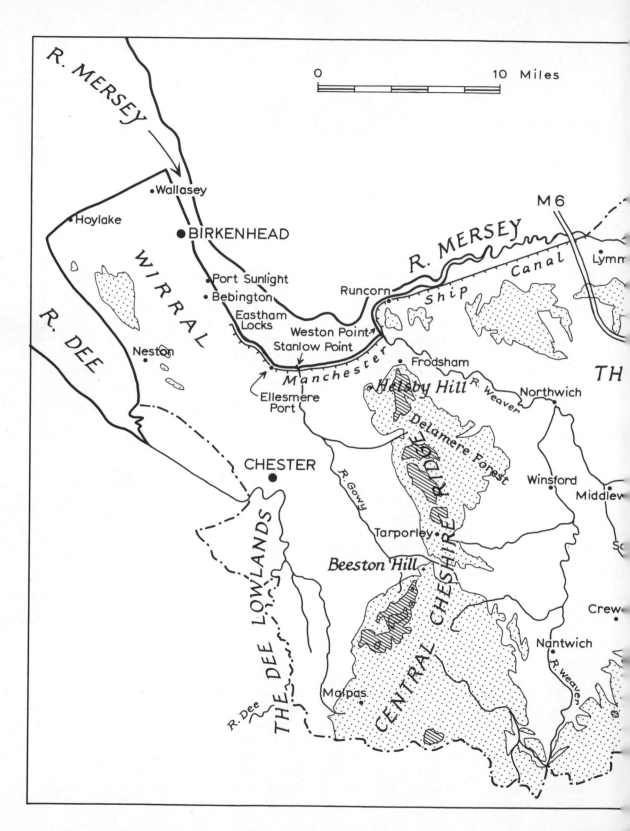

2. SURFA

Stalybridge

•Mottram

Hyde

Sale

R. Goyt

STOCKPORT

rincham

Marple

THE PENNINE EDGE

•Wilmslow

Knutsford

EAST

ESHIRE

Macclesfield

Dane

Shuttlings
Low

PLAIN

Congleton

Cloud End

Mow Cop

M 6

HEIGHT IN FEET

	0
	200
	400
	600
	800
	1000

lower courses of the Dee, the Mersey and the Weaver and especially of the estuaries of the first two, together with the exploitation of salt in the Weaver basin, eventually brought trade and an extension of industry to Cheshire. In the eighteenth and nineteenth centuries the building of canals and the Weaver Navigation and finally the opening of the Manchester Ship Canal served to underline the economic importance of these major valleys and the estuarine shores. Population found new centres and grew rapidly.

Apart from the high hills of the Pennine Edge and the narrower and less formidable obstacle of the Central Ridge, the entire county is broadly suitable for land transport. Further, it lies across the route from London and the south-east to North Wales and north-west England via the Midland Gap, and from the West of England to the North-west: facts which have closely affected both its history and its importance in the road and rail system of Britain.

By no means one of the largest counties (1,015 square miles), its comparatively cool, northerly climate and heavy woodland cover combined with its relative remoteness from the south of England to delay its development. By the early nineteenth century these drawbacks had been overcome to a large degree and in 1961 its total population was between one and a quarter and one and a half million (1,368,000), its industries numerous and diverse, and its communications and transport highly developed and efficient.

III

Prehistoric Cheshire

The dawn of history in Britain came only with the Roman invasions, but for thousands of years before that Man had slowly been penetrating northward into Britain. His first appearance in what is now Cheshire was long delayed by the great ice sheets which severely limited human movement during the four major phases of the Quaternary Ice Age. Many evidences of Old Stone Age (Palaeolithic) occupation have been found in the south of England, especially from the inter-glacial periods, but so far none has been discovered in Cheshire except for one worked flake found in St. John Street, Chester.

The first main movement northwards began about 8000 B.C. and at some time between that date and 5000 B.C. hunter-fishermen of the Middle Stone Age (Mesolithic) left traces in Wirral and on the Central Cheshire Ridge in the form of tiny stone implements or microliths.

From approximately 3000 B.C. in a mild, wet climatic period woodland spread over Britain, and men of the New Stone Age (Neolithic) reached Cheshire. They used stone axes made in Penmaenmawr and Great Langdale, but whether they were settlers or only traders passing through is uncertain and no settlements of this period have been found here. It is from the drier Bronze Age, about 1750–1550 B.C., that the fairly numerous tumuli or burial mounds scattered over the county, indicate a genuine and rapidly extending settlement of the area, and several types of Bronze Age implements have been found. These folk clearly preferred the comparative safety and wide views of the more open uplands and of patches of sandstone and light sandy soils in the lowlands. There, wild beasts could not lurk unseen as easily as in the woodlands of the wide clay plains, and it is on the Pennine Edge, the Central Ridge and on spreads of glacial sands such as that between Macclesfield and the Dane valley where most Bronze Age implements and tumuli are found. Nevertheless, the occupation of Cheshire at that time in no way compares with the density of settlement in the Clwydian Heights to the west or the High Peak to the east.

Stone axes and the relatively soft bronze implements allow only slow woodland clearance, with fire as Man's second ally for this purpose, hence economic activities were very restricted until iron was introduced. The Neolithic period is only thinly represented in Cheshire but we have one chambered tomb —the Bridestones near Congleton. The people of both the Neolithic and Bronze cultures were farmers raising crops and farm animals. The people of both cultures made pottery and knew the art of weaving, and the Bronze Age people were, of course, metal workers but, with the introduction of iron using from the Continent in the mid-sixth century B.C., the whole picture changed. The hard cutting edge of the new axes made possible the first extensive advance into the woodlands; iron ploughshares turned up more ground for food crops and, despite the wet phase which encouraged the further spread of woodland, Man made real progress in clearing and settling the hillsides and even the lowlands. Iron and timber came into general use for building more commodious dwellings, for domestic fittings and tools; and pottery, skins, woven cloth, personal ornaments, and an increasing supply of food and goods all contributed to a more secure and comfortable life and to the increase of population in the Early Iron Age. These invaders from Europe also brought with them the Brythonic language, a branch of Old Celtic and themselves are known as Celts. Finds from this period in Cheshire are still relatively few, but there are two main clues to the areas they occupied. The first is the group of seven hill forts, all on or near the Central Ridge. The largest of these are the double-ditched or multivallate forts of Helsby Hill, Eddisbury, and Maiden Castle (Bickerton), though they do not bear comparison with great forts such as Old Oswestry or Moel Hiraddug. Only Oakmere is on low ground. The rest command wide views and were obviously used for defence. The huts excavated at Eddisbury give an idea of the primitive dwellings.

The second key to the Celtic settlement sites is afforded by place-names, and many Celtic place-names and place-name elements survive in Cheshire: many more must certainly have been lost or replaced by later ones. Crewe, Wheelock, Landican, and Ince (this last Goidelic) are Celtic names, and other elements include *dun* and *pen*. The

Celtic settlement was well established by the time the Romans came and it lasted throughout the Romano-British period (these Celts were the British or Brythons) and they remained virtually undisturbed until the Anglian incursions which, in the Welsh Borderland, date only from approximately A.D. 600. The British of the northern Borderland were known to the Romans as the Cornovii and as the *Pax Romana* was established (or enforced!), there appears to have been a movement down from the hill forts, but even in the lowlands, these people built on high points for preference. Dunham on the Hill and Barrow are fine examples and so are a group of hamlets west of Maiden Castle. Trackways increased in number and many of these seem to be indicated by place-names, though roads offer many problems of dating. So from the Early Iron Age with its Celtic culture and its Brythonic or British people and language, can be traced the first extensive bases of the human geography of present day Cheshire.

IV

The Romans in Cheshire

After the abortive attempts to conquer Britain under Julius Caesar in 55 and 54 B.C., the Romans again landed in Kent under the Emperor Claudius in A.D. 43. By A.D. 47, they had occupied the south and east of England as far as a line joining Gloucester (Glevum) and Lincoln (Lindum) and these two places together with Wroxeter (Viroconium) near Shrewsbury were legionary fortresses in the early phase.

The advance northward and westward was by no means even or uninterrupted for it then approached the difficult Highland Zone, and it was from that time that the Cheshire lowlands, lying between the Brigantian territory of the Pennines and the Ordovices and the Deceangli of North Wales, became strategically important to the Romans. Paulinus marched against Anglesey in A.D. 60 (or 61) and probably used Chester (Deva) as his base. But the main occupation of Cheshire took place after north-eastern England had been made secure by setting up the legionary fortress of York.

In A.D. 74 after Frontinus had subdued the Silures of South Wales, he turned his attention to the Ordovices. Caerleon (Isca) superseded Gloucester as the frontier was shifted westward and about A.D. 45 the building of the legionary fortress of Chester was begun. So York, Chester and Caerleon replaced the earlier legionary fortresses. Agricola completed the subjugation of the Ordovices and, with Roman power firmly established along the length of the Cambrian border, Chester was supplied with piped water by A.D. 79 and was manned by the Second Legion until this was replaced by the Twentieth in about A.D. 86–7.

Chester has many advantages as a settlement site. It is at the lowest bridging point of the River Dee and in Roman times and in the early Middle Ages the broad tidal waters swept up over what is now the Roodee to afford the best port facilities north of Bristol. Low sandstone bluffs on either side of the river offer a dry, elevated site for building; the same sandstones here and nearby provide good building stone; and the river- and well-water is abundant. The trade of the port of Chester was considerable in the Roman period and from the third century the place had added value in coastal defence against Irish pirates.

The early fort had consisted of wooden buildings within a turf wall but soon after A.D. 100 a stone wall was erected and stone or stone and timber buildings replaced the earlier ones. At its height, the fortress housed over 5,000 soldiers but in periods of relative peace the complement fell to about 1,000. Outside the fortress and principally on its eastern side was the civil settlement. The layout, buildings, roads, life, and equipment of Roman Chester are vividly portrayed in the Grosvenor Museum by means of pictures, models and numerous finds, not to mention the lifelike figure of a Roman legionary. Considerable bits of masonry survive in the city especially near the Wolf Gate at the site of the amphitheatre, which was excavated during the 1960s and is to be opened to the public. In the 1960s further discoveries were made revealing the headquarters building, the legate's palace, a large bath building, barracks, and granaries.

Roman Chester was first and foremost a fortress and a road centre. Major Roman roads connected it with northern Britain, south-eastern Britain, and the Welsh Borderland, and the lesser ones branched off into Wales and various parts of Cheshire.

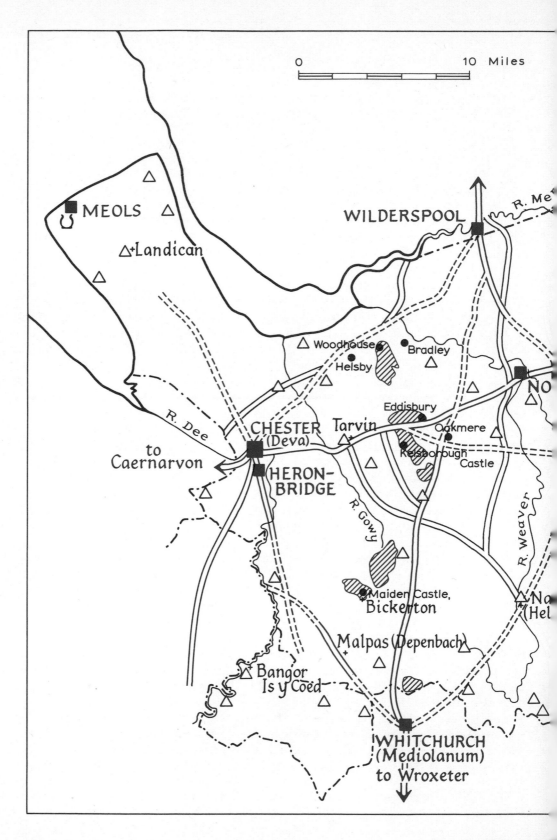

0   10 Miles

■ MEOLS

△ Landican

WILDERSPOOL ■

R. Me

△ Woodhouse ● Bradley
● Helsby

NO ■

Eddisbury
CHESTER ● Oakmere
(Deva) Tarvin
to Kelsborough
Caernarvon Castle
■ HERON-
BRIDGE

R. Dee R. Gowy R. Weaver

Maiden Castle, Na
Bickerton (Hel

Malpas (Depenbach)

Bangor
Is y Coed

■ WHITCHURCH
(Mediolanum)
to Wroxeter

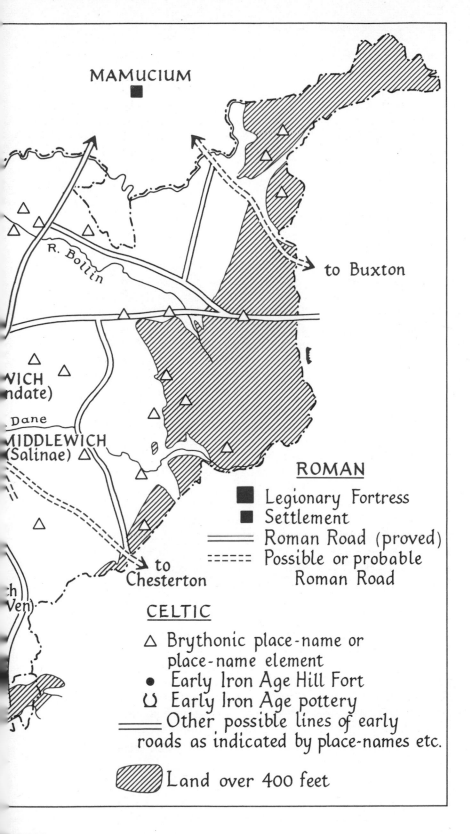

MAMUCIUM

to Buxton

R. Bollin

WICH
(ndate)

Dane

MIDDLEWICH
(Salinae)

to
Chesterton

h
Ven)

ROMAN

■ Legionary Fortress
■ Settlement
══ Roman Road (proved)
- - - - Possible or probable
  Roman Road

CELTIC

△ Brythonic place-name or
  place-name element
● Early Iron Age Hill Fort
∪ Early Iron Age pottery
── Other possible lines of early
roads as indicated by place-names etc.

▨ Land over 400 feet

Near to Chester were three dependent Roman settlements: Saltney, two miles to the south-west on the south bank of the Dee estuary, probably an agricultural settlement; Heron-bridge two miles to the south on the left bank of the river, partly a metal-working site but also used for transhipment of goods from Holt to complete their journey to Chester by road; and Holt itself, some seven miles up-stream from Chester, producing the tiles and pottery. The metal workers were in Deva itself.

Beyond these, the best known Roman site in Cheshire is Wilderspool from which a dry approach across the Mersey marshes could be made to the ford across that river. It was thus a vital point in northward communications. It is now crossed by the line of the Manchester Ship Canal and it was during the excavation of the canal bed that the first Roman discoveries were made. These included hearths and furnaces thought to have been used for glass and metal production. In recent excavations, large timber buildings have been traced. If at first Wilderspool was a small fortress, it became more important later as a crossing point and industrial centre, the latter function shared by Stockton Heath.

At Northwich (believed to be the Condate of the Antonine Itinerary) the Dane joins the River Weaver and a little to the east the Watling Street which goes from Chester to Manchester (Mamucium) crosses King Street, part of the great Roman route northward across Lancashire, and south to the Welsh border and south-east to London. Both Northwich and Middlewich (Salinae), where the last two routes diverge, may have been of use to the Romans for their salt. The nature of the settlements still remains largely enig-matic, but the recent finds, including a soldier's helmet, suggest that Condate may have begun as a fort.

Meols on the north coast of Wirral has a proved Roman occupation layer above the considerable prehistoric remains, but although there are several other quite strong possibilities no other Roman settlement in Cheshire has so far been proved. Nantwich midway between Middlewich and Whit-church seems the strongest candidate.

Not far outside the county boundary Manchester, Whitchurch (Mediolanum), Chesterton (in Staffordshire), Pentre and Ffrith in Flintshire each lay on a road from Chester and beyond these, York (Eboracum), Lancaster, Caerleon (Isca), and London were among the far-flung points linked to Chester by Rome's great military highways.

By no means all the 'probable' lines of Roman roads either in or beyond Cheshire are as yet proven, and excavation continues actively in many parts, its exciting results con-stantly revealing more and more of the geo-graphy of Roman Britain and of the life and economy of its people. In the Roman towns and in the villas (of which last Cheshire has none), the standard of life was similar to that of the great urban civilizations of Rome and its Mediterranean colonies and, although the character of everyday life among the Celtic folk of the north and west of Britain lagged far behind this, they gained considerably from contacts which lasted nearly 400 years.

When Rome finally withdrew from Britain in A.D. 410 because of the Asiatic hordes threatening the Empire and when, in the same period, the barbarians from the Euro-pean continent were raiding the shores of eastern and southern Britain, it was the Celtic people who carried the Roman torch and made possible the survival of Christian-ity and of many features of Latin culture through the Dark Ages. Agriculture and communications and the general standard of living had all improved during the *Pax Romana*, and the main geographical heritage in Cheshire was Chester and the network of Roman roads.

V

The Anglian and Scandinavian Settlement of Cheshire

Looking back to the history of Cheshire in the Dark Ages it seems very dark indeed. Only six Cheshire places are mentioned in the *Anglo-Saxon Chronicle*, the chief source of the general history of the period, and the area figures even less in Bede's *Ecclesiastical History of the English Nation* for Cheshire was near the margins of the area served by the Celtic Church, and came late under the influence of the Roman Church. There are few historical events in Cheshire which can be deemed certain apart from the Battle of Chester, but place-names make it possible to reconstruct a remarkable part of the progress of settlement within the county.

By A.D. 600, the Anglo-Saxons were firmly in control of southern and eastern England and much of the Midlands, but the west of Britain from Glasgow down to Cornwall was still a British terrain. The British (or Welsh) who were well versed in the arts and had long been Christian, were tribal pastoralists, living in hamlets and scattered dwellings in both the hills and the lowlands. By contrast the Anglo-Saxons (or English), though advancing in craftsmanship, were still by no means all Christian, and were an agricultural peasantry, unlettered and living in villages and hamlets, but their leaders had political and administrative ability. During the early seventh century, two large Anglian kingdoms were pressing towards Cheshire. Northumbria, which included the area north of the Humber, had expanded across the Pennines into Cumbria and from there southwards towards the Mersey, while the great Midland kingdom of Mercia was advancing into the borders of what is now Wales, catching Cheshire in a pincer movement.

About the year 613, the Northumbrians descended on the rich, fertile plains of the lower Dee and engaged the British in a pitched battle near Chester which the Venerable Bede described vividly in these words:

' . . . the warlike king of the English, Ethelfrid . . . having raised a mighty army, made a very great slaughter of that perfidious nation (the British), at the City of Legions (Chester). . . . Being about to give battle, he observed their priests, who were come together to offer up their prayers to God for the soldiers, standing apart in a place of safety . . . Most of them were of the monastery of Bangor . . . Many of these . . . resorted among others to pray at the aforesaid battle . . . to defend them against the swords of the barbarians. King Ethelfrid being informed of the occasion of their coming said, "if then they cry to their God against us, in truth, though they do not bear arms, yet they fight against us, because they oppose us by their prayers." He therefore commanded them to be attacked first, and then destroyed with the rest of the impious army, not without considerable loss of his own forces.'

The Northumbrian army followed up the victory by marching further up the Dee valley and razing to the ground the great churches and libraries and other monastic buildings at Bangor-on-Dee, and to this day no trace of them has been found. But the Northumbrian triumph was short-lived. So, some twenty-five years later, was that of their Christian King Oswald who marched across Cheshire to defeat the pagan King Penda of Mercia near the town which is still called after him—Oswestry.

When the English reached the Welsh Borderland, their early land-hunger was largely satisfied, and their motives for winning

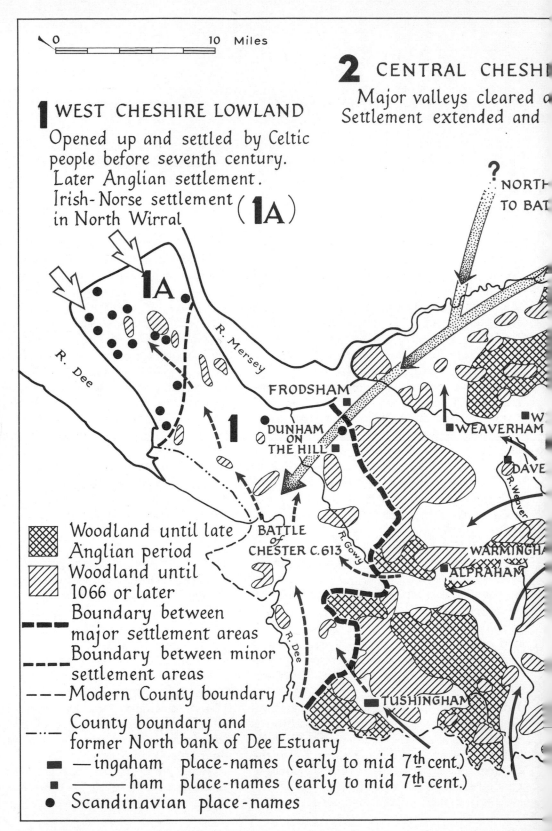

1 WEST CHESHIRE LOWLAND
Opened up and settled by Celtic
people before seventh century.
Later Anglian settlement.
Irish-Norse settlement
in North Wirral (**1A**)

2 CENTRAL CHESHI
Major valleys cleared a
Settlement extended and

? NORTH
TO BAT

R. Mersey

R. Dee

R. Dee

R. Gowy

R. Weaver

FRODSHAM

DUNHAM ON THE HILL

1

1A

BATTLE of CHESTER C.613

WEAVERHAM

W

DAVE

WARMINGHA

ALPRAHAM

TUSHINGHAM

0 — 10 Miles

Woodland until late Anglian period

Woodland until 1066 or later

Boundary between major settlement areas

Boundary between minor settlement areas

Modern County boundary

County boundary and former North bank of Dee Estuary

■—ingaham place-names (early to mid 7th cent.)

■——ham place-names (early to mid 7th cent.)

● Scandinavian place-names

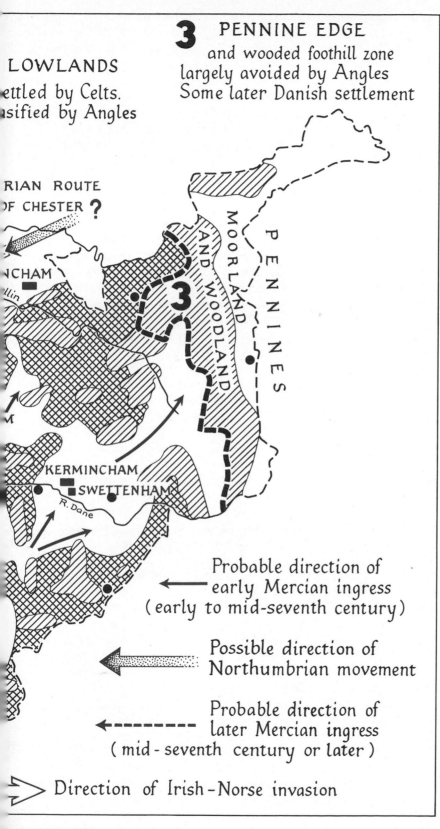

3 PENNINE EDGE
and wooded foothill zone
largely avoided by Angles
Some later Danish settlement

LOWLANDS
...ttled by Celts.
...sified by Angles

...RIAN ROUTE
...OF CHESTER **?**

...NCHAM

...llin

MOORLAND AND WOODLAND

PENNINES

3

KERMINCHAM
SWETTENHAM
R. Dane

Probable direction of
early Mercian ingress
(early to mid-seventh century)

Possible direction of
Northumbrian movement

Probable direction of
later Mercian ingress
(mid-seventh century or later)

Direction of Irish-Norse invasion

new territory were mainly political. By the time they reached Cheshire, the south and east of Britain had been English for the better part of two centuries and the numbers of colonists who filtered into these cooler, northern plains were small. Nothing is recorded of battles between the British and the Mercians in this area, and they probably moved quietly into the Cheshire plains, establishing some sort of control over the lesser places, but settling mainly in the larger ones. As further evidence of their peaceful coexistence, in 633 they marched side by side against the Northumbrians.

The earliest points at which the Anglo-Saxons settled in any district can be traced by the element *ingas* or *ingaham* when it is part of a place-name. There are no *ing* names in Cheshire but there are four *ingham* endings. One is Altrincham in the Mersey valley, and and it may have been an early Northumbrian settlement *or* a Mercian one. The other three are Mercian. They are Tushingham in the Malpas area on a route which led directly to the fertile lower Dee valley; Warmingham in the valley of Wheelock brook in mid-Cheshire near the good lands of the middle Weaver basin; and Kermincham not far to the east in the Dane valley. From these, expansion took place, first to *ham*, and then to *ingatun* or *ington* settlements. Later came the *-tun* or *-ton* names which are most numerous of the early Anglo-Saxon suffixes in Cheshire. These were all probably in existence by the end of the eighth century. A number of churches, such as Bunbury, Astbury, Prestbury, and Wybunbury have the early Anglo-Saxon suffix *burh* (bury) which was applied to fortified places of any age. In addition, the churches are built on elevated sites. This lends strength to the supposition that many of the old parochial centres of Cheshire were pre-existing British settlements, some perhaps places where there had been an ancient Celtic church. Finally, the Mercians pushed their way into the unsettled woodlands and heaths as all the land cleared by the British had been taken over by the end of the *-tun* phase. This

last period of colonization can be traced by the *leah* (ley) names (meaning a clearing) and *wood* names and the areas involved are marked on the map in cross shading. They are particularly numerous around the medieval forests of Delamere and Macclesfield.

The long peaceful years of the ninth century during which the late Mercian hamlets were founded and the older villages and hamlets expanded, were rudely ended by the invasions and threats of invasions by the Vikings. There were two Scandinavian colonizations of Cheshire: that of the Irish-Norse who came into Wirral from Dublin; and that of the Danes who occupied a comparatively small number of places in east Cheshire and adjoining parts of south-east Lancashire. The Irish-Norse came over from Ireland between 870 and 924, first raiding, then 'wintering' and settling in Wirral. There were already Celtic and English places here in abundance, and the Norse added a third set of place-names such as *Irby*, Whit*by*, *Kirby*, Greas*by*, *Thing*wall (*thing* indicating that it was a place of government), and *Thur*staston ('the stone of the pagan god Thor'). This second pagan invasion again set civilization back for a time, but before the Norman Conquest the Norse had not only become Christians but were important landowners and traders in Cheshire to which they introduced the duodecimal system of coinage.

A much thinner stream of Danes reached east Cheshire, their settlements traceable in such place-names as Cheadle *Hulme*, *Holmes* Chapel (formerly Church *Hulme*), *Scholar* Green (thought to derive from Skali, a Scandinavian proper name), *Toft*, and Rostherne. They came during the early part of the tenth century when the Danelagh—the kingdom established by the Danes in eastern England and the east Midlands—was attempting to press its conquests still further into western Mercia. Between A.D. 913 and 919, Aethelfleda, Lady of the Mercians and daughter of Alfred the Great, organized the building of a chain of forts from Cheshire far south into the Borderland. Eddisbury, the

1. Beeston Castle and the Cheshire Plain from Peckforton Castle.

2. Diorama of Roman Chester.

3. Sandbach: The Saxon Crosses, now in the market place.

Early Iron Age camp, was re-fortified in 914, the fort of Runcorn built in 915, and Thelwall in 919. There was a second Danish raid into Cheshire in 980, and there is a tradition that *Knuts*ford was named after Canute's forces had crossed the stream there. In 1016, a joint army went forth against the Danes from Cheshire, Shropshire and Staffordshire, but by 1017 the worst of the Scandinavian menace was over.

The whole of England was slowly integrated into a single state, and although the dwellings of the peasantry remained poor, most people were better off, agriculture was extending, and the majority of the villages and hamlets were firmly established. Chester which, in 893 had been nothing but 'a deserted Roman site in Wirral' as we read in the *Anglo-Saxon Chronicle*, was rebuilt in 907 according to that same Chronicle. From then onward, the City of the Legions was a shire town and began to regain its old importance as a road centre. Traffic increased in its port, and it was there that Edgar, after his crowning at Bath, received six kings who came to pay homage to him.

VI

Cheshire under the Earls

After the coronation of William the Conqueror in Westminster Abbey on Christmas Day 1066, he made numerous progresses through the country to display his power and survey his kingdom. In the first years of his reign, rebellions sprang up in the Fens and in Yorkshire, and in 1069 Chester and Shrewsbury rose in revolt against the Norman yoke. So, fresh from pillaging and subduing Yorkshire, William marched with his armies across the Pennines in the bitter cold of the winter of 1069–70 entering Cheshire via the 'pan handle' north-east of Stockport. His routes to Chester and Shrewsbury were strewn with 'wasted' manors, still traceable across the county by plotting the waste recorded in 1086 in the Domesday Book. The strongholds of Stockport and Macclesfield lay in ruins, and those of the people of the eastern plains who were not killed fled westward for safety, leaving most of east Cheshire desolate for many a year.

With Chester subdued, the Anglo-Saxon Earl Edwin of Mercia was replaced by the Norman Gherbod as Earl of Chester in 1070 but his tenure was brief and ineffective. Not so that of his successor Hugh d'Avranches known also as Hugh Lupus or, because he was grossly overweight, as Hugh the Fat. The power of the earls was semi-regal and the county became the Palatine County of Chester although the term 'palatinate' (meaning palace or independent government) did not appear in documents until 1297. The task of the earls was both to rule Cheshire and to advance the conquest into Wales. H. J. Hewitt summarized the role of medieval Cheshire in this way: 'a territorial unit existing for a military purpose, standing between England and Wales, being part of neither'. England lay 'beyond the Lyme' and the Cheshire barons owed the earl no military service outside the county. In fact, however, Cheshire men were for centuries involved in wars and her archers were the finest in the land.

Until 1284, the river Clwyd was considered to be the western boundary of the county and one of Earl Hugh's first acts was to send his cousin Robert to be Lord of Rhuddlan at the mouth of that river. Only after Robert of Rhuddlan's death was the Earl himself invested with the task of pushing forward the attack on Wales.

Until 1237 when the earldom passed into royal hands, Cheshire was ruled by the Norman Earls of Chester under whom were eight barons. Each of these was given a great estate on which he built his baronial seat, maintained armed men, held his own baronial court and, in many cases, these barons founded towns and chartered markets and fairs. The Baron of Halton was also Constable of Cheshire, and the Baron of Montalt whose castle was at Mold was Hereditary Seneschal or High Steward of the county. The remaining six, distributed at strategic points, were the Malbengs of Wich Malbedeng (Nantwich), the Baron of Malpas (FitzHugh in the first instance), the Vernons of Shipbrook, the Masseys of Dunham Massey, the Venables of Kinderton, and at some date a baron of Stockport, but this barony died out.

The administration of the county was carried out by a multiplicity of officers with characteristic Norman thoroughness and complexity, and many of these officers continued for centuries and not a few to the present day. These included the High Justiciary, the Sheriff, the Ballivi or bailiffs (the Sergeants of the Peace, the Foresters of

Wirral, Mara, and Macclesfield, and the Bailiffs of Northwich and Macclesfield), the Chamberlain who presided in the Court of the Exchequer and many lesser officials. The highest court was that of the Earl, below which came the baronial courts, the courts leet, and the manorial courts.

The Earl held his land direct from the King, the Barons from the Earl and the Lords of the lesser manors from the Barons. So vast were the holdings of the earls that at one time they were said to comprise an area equivalent to one-third of the whole of England. The hierarchical structure of feudalism was evident in every division of society —the aristocracy, the Church, the army, and the commoners. In turn it was reflected in landholding and the Norman adage '*Nulle terre sans seigneur*' (No land without a lord) meant the replacement of the relatively democratic Anglo-Saxon township by the manor and the subservience of the tenants to its lord. Resentment flared in all ranks and even the barons complained of oppression. As a result of the barons' demands, Earl Ranulf III drew up the *Carta Communis Cestriensis*— the 'Magna Carta of Cheshire'—in 1215–16, which granted some of the privileges demanded and refused others—among these last being the right to shoot in the earl's forests or to feed their swine there. Henceforth, however, they could try most cases in their own courts, allow strangers to settle on their land, assart lands in the arable area of the forests, and take wood from them for the building and repair of houses and fences.

After the devastation of 1069–70, recovery was at first slow, but as Chester arose from the ashes of the Dark Ages as a great military base, port, and market and as baronial and lesser castles and new towns were built, trade and production reached new heights and the population increased. In the countryside, the small villages and the little hamlets recovered and grew under the Norman lords who, if they were autocratic, were also keen to enhance the economy. Until the end of the thirteenth century, military considerations were a matter of priority. Major castles were erected at Chester, Frodsham, Halton, Dunham Massey, Stockport, Macclesfield, Malpas, Nantwich, and Shotwick. In the thirteenth century, the mighty stronghold of Beeston came into being to control the vital Beeston Gap and, in what is now Flintshire, Rhuddlan castle was rebuilt, Flint was planned as a castle town and a number of lesser castles were built or strengthened at vital defensive points along the Clwyd and the land to the east. New roads were cut for military purposes across Flintshire and, although the surfaces were everywhere appalling, some attempts were made to improve them for the passage of trade and armed men.

In the first half of the fourteenth century a period of peace brought relief to the war-weary county, though from that time the importance of Chester as a military base declined and brought other and adverse effects to bear. There is no precise source of population figures for these early periods, but it has been estimated that in 1086 there were about 11,000 people in Cheshire. During the thirteenth and fourteenth centuries there are records of 2, 3, and 4,000 Cheshire footmen and archers serving in various campaigns which suggests that the total population must by the early fourteenth century have been many thousands.

When the prospects seemed fairer than since the early Norman era, disaster struck in common with the rest of the country in the shape of the dreaded plague or Black Death. In 1349 and some later years it reached all parts of the country and the number of deaths was so great that it is estimated that, from a population of about 4 million, the total for England dropped to about $2\frac{1}{2}$ million. The beginning of the Hundred Years War had again taken Cheshire's skilled archers to the field of battle and it was only towards the end of the Middle Ages that the county could once more claim a measure of prosperity.

A century before the Black Death, in 1237,

John le Scot the last of the line of Norman earls of Chester had died and the earldom passed into royal hands. Edward I bestowed it on his son Edward of Caernarvon (later Edward II) who was thus the first of the continuing line of Princes of Wales to become the Earl of Chester. The title has ever since been conferred on the heir to the throne and, because of this, the Chester Herald was present at the Investiture of H.R.H. Prince Charles as Prince of Wales at Caernarvon in July 1969.

VII

Cheshire and the Welsh Wars

The fate of Chester after the withdrawal of Rome is shrouded in mist, but Cheshire remained Celtic until the beginning of the seventh century. It was probably part of the Welsh kingdom of Powys, and Chester is said to have been one of its capitals. Even after the Anglo-Saxon settlement when Cheshire became part of Mercia and was no longer British or Welsh politically, it was linked with North Wales during the alliance of Mercia with Gwynedd. But during the latter half of the eighth century the boundary between the Welsh Uplands and the English Plain was marked by Offa's Dyke. Power see-sawed back and forth across the upland edge until the Union of England and Wales in 1536, and Chester functioned time and again as one of the principal military bases of the Welsh Borderland. From this city the armies of Cheshire and of England set out to the Welsh wars, and to it they fell back.

The pattern of border warfare had been set before the Norman Conquest. For example, in the eleventh century Gruffydd ap Llewelyn, prince of Gwynedd and possibly also of Powys, campaigned against the English. By 1044, he ruled most of Wales and for nearly twenty years, often in alliance with Mercia, he raided the lowlands. In 1062, however, Earl Harold with Mercian agreement rode to Chester and to Gruffydd's palace at Rhuddlan, and the next year ravaged North Wales. Gruffydd was killed by one of his own men in that same year but he had so inspired the Welsh that, by the time the Normans arrived, they found a largely united Wales instead of a series of minor kingdoms.

When Edwin earl of Mercia was replaced in 1070 by the Norman Gherbod as Earl of Chester and in the following year by Hugh Lupus, the long peaceful alliance between Mercia and the Welsh was over. The Normans were determined to conquer Wales and to that end the Welsh Borderland was marshalled into a series of marcher lordships geared for war. At the northern end of the border with Chester as the key to the North Welsh routes, the earldom was of major importance in this plan and for over two hundred years knew little peace. The Normans were far ahead of the Welsh and the Anglo-Saxons in the art of war: their castles stronger, their men better protected and equipped. Earl Hugh was given full powers for the promotion of the war against Wales, and as a first move, he sent his cousin Robert to be lord of Rhuddlan thus securing the line of the river Clwyd and confirming the Flintshire area as part of Cheshire. From Rhuddlan, the Normans advanced across the Denbighshire coastlands, built a castle at Deganwy and, with the aid of the exiled prince of Gwynedd, Gruffydd ap Cynan, Earl Hugh had conquered Gwynedd before his death in 1088.

Soon Gruffydd turned on his Norman allies, but he was captured and taken in chains to Chester castle where he languished as a prisoner for many years. Eventually he was rescued by one of his own countrymen, and became one of the great leaders of his people. From 1100 to 1114 he ruled Gwynedd and north-east Wales, recovering the land between the Dee and the Clwyd which in 1086 was recorded with Cheshire in the Domesday Book. So he closed the first phase of Norman occupation of the Borderland.

North Wales revolted again during the reign of Henry I, and during that of his successor Henry II a further invasion was

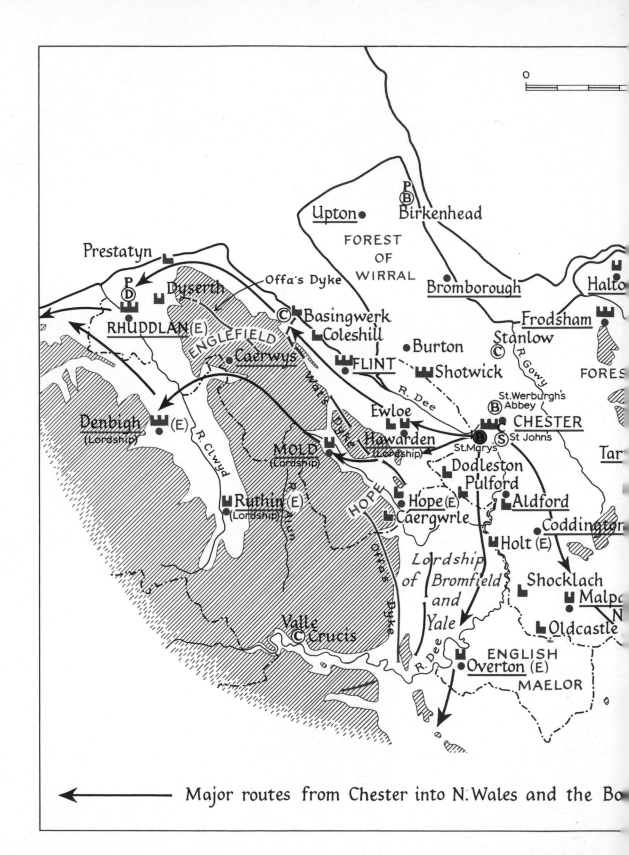

Prestatyn

Upton

P Ⓑ Birkenhead

FOREST OF WIRRAL

Offa's Dyke

Bromborough

Halto

P Ⓓ Dyserth

RHUDDLAN (E)

Ⓒ Basingwerk
Coleshill

Burton

Frodsham

Stanlow

FORES

ENGLEFIELD

Caerwys

FLINT

Shotwick

Ⓒ R. Gowy

Denbigh
(Lordship)

(E)

R. Clwyd

Wat's Dyke

R. Dee

Ewloe

St. Werburgh's Abbey

Ⓑ

CHESTER

Ⓑ

Ⓢ St Johns

Ⓢ St. Marys

MOLD
(Lordship)

Hawarden
(Lordship)

Tar

HOPE

Dodleston
Pulford

Ruthin (E)
(Lordship)

Hope (E)

Caergwrle

Aldford

Coddington

Offa's Dyke

Holt (E)

Lordship of Bromfield and Yale

Shocklach

Malp

N

Valle Ⓒ Crucis

R. Dee

Oldcastle

ENGLISH

Overton (E)

MAELOR

←——————— Major routes from Chester into N. Wales and the Bo

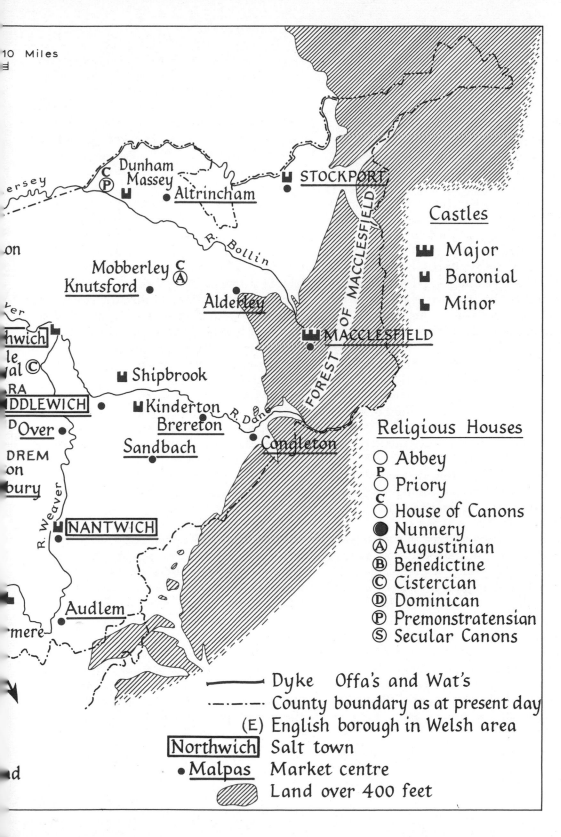

10 Miles

Castles

⌗ Major
⌐ Baronial
⌐ Minor

Dunham Massey
C
P
Altrincham
STOCKPORT

R. Bollin

Mobberley C
Knutsford A
Alderley
MACCLESFIELD

FOREST OF MACCLESFIELD

Shipbrook

Kinderton
Brereton
Sandbach
R. Dan
Congleton

Religious Houses

○ Abbey
Ⓟ○ Priory
Ⓒ○ House of Canons
● Nunnery
Ⓐ Augustinian
Ⓑ Benedictine
Ⓒ Cistercian
Ⓓ Dominican
Ⓟ Premonstratensian
Ⓢ Secular Canons

hwich
le
al C
RA
DDLEWICH
D Over
DREM
on
bury
R. Weaver
NANTWICH

Audlem
mere

————— Dyke Offa's and Wat's
—·—·— County boundary as at present day
(E) English borough in Welsh area
Northwich Salt town
• Malpas Market centre
▨ Land over 400 feet

mounted, Rhuddlan captured, Gwynedd invaded, and the submission secured of Llewelyn ap Iorwerth, prince of Gwynedd. The pendulum of war continued to swing to and fro across the border, with Cheshire's archers always ready for action, but the time came when King John, preoccupied with the War of the Barons, gave Llewelyn a further chance to become master of Wales. In 1218, Llewelyn concluded an agreement with Ranulf III, Earl of Chester, that the lordships of Mold and Englefield should belong to Gwynedd and that his daughter Helen should marry Ranulf's son John le Scot, who became the last Norman Earl of Chester before the earldom reverted to the Crown. Peace reigned again, but of the Welsh lands only Hawarden remained to Cheshire.

Earl John died in 1237 and in 1240 trouble once more broke out in North Wales. Henry III assembled an army at Chester, restored Englefield to the Crown and Mold to Roger de Montalt, the latter only to be lost to Dafydd ap Llewelyn two years later. Prestatyn and Dyserth castles were destroyed and never rebuilt. War continued intermittently and when the Treaty of Montgomery was signed in 1267, Hawarden was again all that Cheshire could claim in Wales.

Only a few years elapsed before the so-called Wars of Welsh Independence (1276–7 and 1282–3). They were waged in the reign of Edward I, the greatest strategist since the time of William the Conqueror. In Chester were stored vast amounts of corn from Ireland and many English counties. Carts and wagons were chartered to transfer food and equipment to the city. New roads were cut across Flintshire and preparations made to build the castle and town of Flint. This was the age of the great *bastides* or *villes neuves*, the 'new defended towns' originated on the continent, and before the turn of the century Edward I fortified the whole of North Wales from Hawarden to Conway with his magnificent castles and walled boroughs. A new castle replaced the old one at Rhuddlan and, with his line secured thus far, the English armies set out from Chester in July 1277 and, advancing on Conway, forced Llewelyn's submission in Snowdonia. The Treaty of Conway gave England all the land to the east of the river of that name.

Despite this, in March 1282 Dafydd ap Gruffydd who had at one time resided in his Cheshire manor of Frodsham, mounted an attack on Rhuddlan, Flint, and Hawarden while his Welsh allies took Ruthin and Hope castles. Although surprised, Edward nevertheless again dispatched his armies across the Dee bridge and rushed in supplies from as far away as Scotland and Gascony. This second war ended in complete victory for the English and, by the treaty of Rhuddlan (1284), five Welsh counties were created in West Wales on the English model and, in the north-east, Flintshire was formed from Englefield, Hope, and Maelor Saesneg, leaving Hawarden and Mold lordships still separate.

It was not always an easy peace that followed, but the major Anglo-Welsh wars were over. Relations with Flintshire had always been good and the close trade links between Cheshire and Flintshire continued. There were only two more serious breaks in the peace between the two countries—the Welsh revolt of 1294–5 and the ill-starred rebellions under Owain Glyndwr from 1400 to 1403. It was again from Chester that Edward I set out in December 1294, but in the fifteenth century revolt Shrewsbury was the more important base.

VIII

The Medieval Countryside

The first precise information about Cheshire agriculture is in the Domesday Book of 1086. In this great record there is information about most places in Cheshire, and when all these are mapped a picture emerges of the extent of woodlands, arable lands, meadows and waste land across the entire width of the county. There were three Forests in Cheshire in the eleventh century: Wirral, Mara and Mondrem, and Macclesfield. These were the hunting grounds of the Earls and included woodland, pasture, waste, and even cultivated fields. Already the Forest of Wirral had little wooded country left in it, Macclesfield was largely wooded on the lower land and some of the hill slopes of of the Pennines, but moorland took its place at higher levels, and Mara and Mondrem (now known as Delamere Forest) was mainly wooded. This last extended between the Gowy and Weaver rivers on the west and east, to the Mersey in the north and towards Nantwich in the south and, like Macclesfield Forest, it covered a huge area.

The devastation caused by the march of William the Conqueror's armies during the midwinter of 1069–70 left much of east Cheshire deserted and even by 1086 the population there was very sparse and few fields were cultivated. The corn and meadow lands at that date were chiefly concentrated in the more densely peopled areas of Wirral, the Dee and Gowy valleys, and the Weaver valley. There were small scattered settlements in south Cheshire between the Weaver and the Dee, but few of any agricultural importance further east.

Here is a typical Domesday entry describing the rich manor of Weaverham in the lower Weaver valley:

Earl Hugh holds Weaverham in demesne. Earl Edwin held it. There are 13 hides geldable. There are 18 ploughlands. There are two ploughs in the demesne and 2 neatherds, 2 serfs and 10 villeins, and 1 bordar and one radman with 1 villein. All together have 3 ploughs. There is a church and a priest, and a mill to serve the hall, and an acre of meadow. A wood 2 leagues long and 1 league broad and 2 hays for roedeer.

The climate of Cheshire was rather too wet for good wheat land but in those days when most farming supplied only local needs every manor grew wheat, barley, and oats of necessity, and ploughed, sowed, and reaped their open fields in common. But the rather small population of most places combined with the Celtic tradition resulted in a field pattern far less regular than that of the two- and three-field townships of the south and east of the country. Varying numbers of small fields were ploughed in Cheshire townships in the Middle Ages, but in Tarvin and Wybunbury (and probably therefore in other manors) a 3-course system was followed in the thirteenth century, that is, two years under grain and the third year fallow for each field, so that there were always two-thirds of the fields bearing crops in any one year.

During the Welsh Wars, much of Cheshire's corn was liable to be commandeered for the army and there were often shortages. Similarly, cattle raised on the rich meadows, on the harvest stubble and in the Forests were taken in large numbers for this purpose. In the thirteenth century, losses were made up by bringing in cattle from Wales, but even after 1284 this movement continued and the reasons for this are not certain. Sheep were bred largely for their wool, but the wool trade was never of importance in the economy of Cheshire, partly on account of the balance of farm economy,

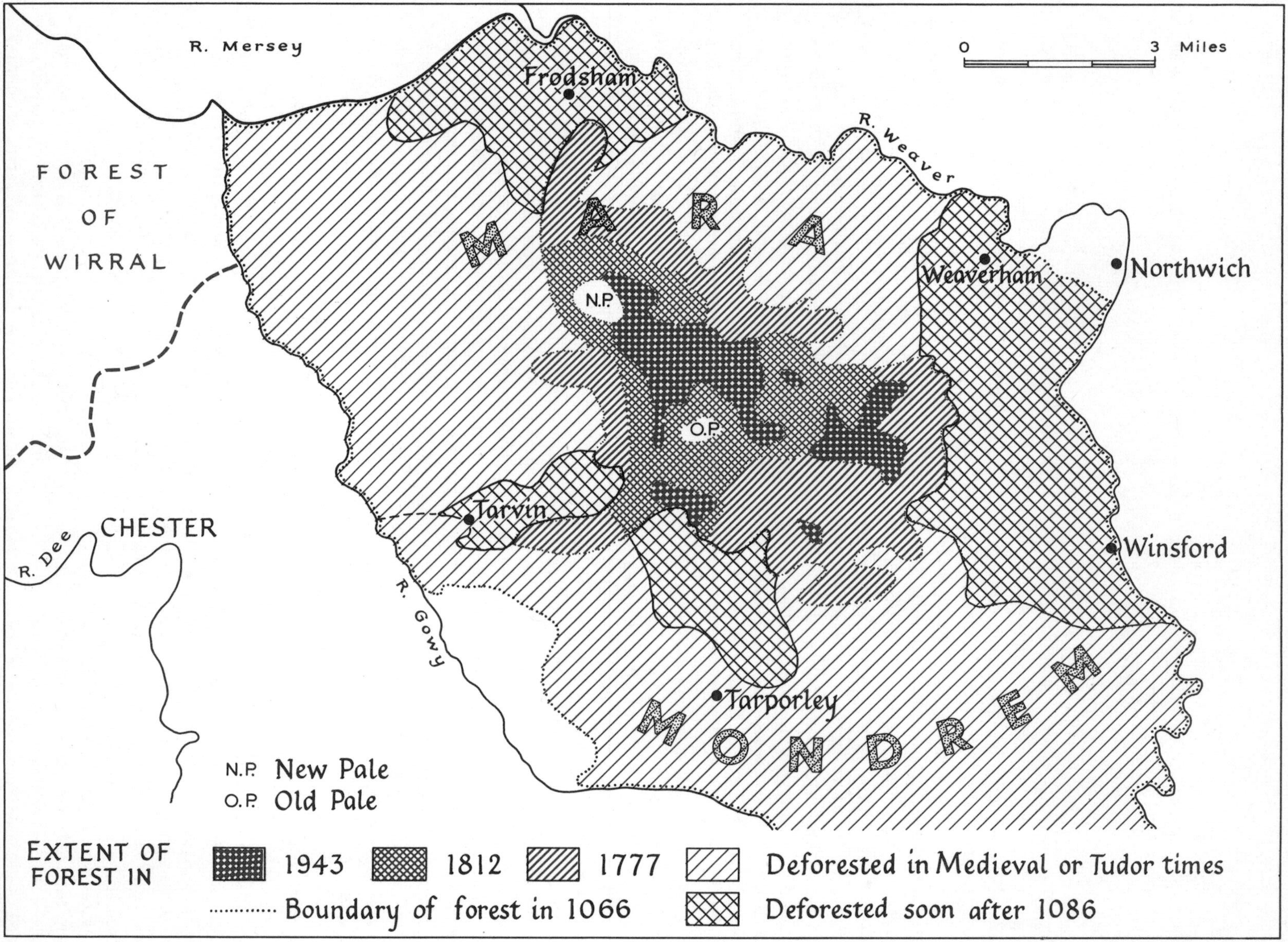

R. Mersey
FOREST OF WIRRAL
Frodsham
R. Weaver
0 3 Miles
MARA
MONDREM
N.P.
O.P.
Weaverham
Northwich
Winsford
Tarvin
CHESTER
R. Dee
R. Gowy
Tarporley
N.P. New Pale
O.P. Old Pale
EXTENT OF FOREST IN
1943
1812
1777
Deforested in Medieval or Tudor times
Boundary of forest in 1066
Deforested soon after 1086

6. DELAMERE FOREST

partly because it was too far from a staple port to make export worth while. The extent of oakwood made acorns so abundant that the raising of pigs was widespread, especially by the lesser folk, in whose diet pork, bacon, and poultry were more important than other flesh meat. The forest laws, however, were harsh and stringent and feeding cattle and pigs within the Forests was closely restricted. So too were the use of timber, the cutting of turves, the taking of honey, the trapping of any animals not classed as vermin, though the woods abounded with deer. The forest courts imposed grim punishments and heavy fines on all who infringed the forest laws. The extent of the Forests was in itself a severe brake on the extension of farming, but enclosure of new land was permitted by the earls and the barons in their woods and wastes from time to time. Similarly, the Abbot of Vale Royal took more land for the plough and by the early fourteenth century many new arable fields had been cut into the eastern fringe of Delamere, most only to be deserted as a result of the Black Death before the century was out. Here, as in the rest of England, there were many vacant tenancies after 1349 as the Black Prince's Register records.

Although the Welsh Wars had ended and, after 1284, there was less border raiding, the French campaigns took many Cheshire men abroad, especially her world famous archers, during the long Hundred Years War sparked off by Edward III's claims to the French throne in 1337. It was the duty of every lord and knight to raise men for the King's army as required. At the battles of Crecy and Poitiers many Cheshire knights fought side by side with the Black Prince. These included Sir Hugh Calveley of Calveley, Sir Hugh

Venables of Kinderton, and the four squires of Lord Audley of Grappenhall—Sir John Delves of Doddington, Sir Robert Foulshurst of Crewe, Sir Thomas Dutton of Dutton, and Sir John Hawkstone of Wrinehill. These four together with the Black Prince and Lord Audley are represented by six battered, life-sized statues round the old tower in Doddington Park. John Delves, knighted in 1347, was given the right to fortify his house at Doddington in 1363. At that time he was buying more land in neighbouring townships, as his successors continued to do during several centuries. It was a typical example of how small estates expanded, some at the expense of tenancies left vacant by death, some by marriage, and some by nibbling into the woodland edges. So the building up of demesne lands, including great parks, was yet another way in which the landscape was being altered during the Middle Ages.

Small, widely spaced parochial villages (and in Wirral a number of non-parochial villages), numerous hamlets, dispersed dwellings, manor houses and their surrounding parks, were dotted over the medieval countryside of Cheshire. Between the richer valley lowlands lay the vast but shrinking Forest of Mara and Mondrem, and to the east the wide woods and moors of Macclesfield Forest. Peat mosses and heaths, some like Rudheath offering sanctuary to escaped criminals, varied the patchwork. As the Middle Ages drew to a close, the standard of housing improved and the characteristic timber-framed manor houses and cottages of the clay lowlands and the sandstone houses of the outcropping hills began to be built, some surviving to this day from the late fifteenth century. Life improved accordingly.

IX

Monasteries and Parishes

The English Church played a major role in the life of the Middle Ages. The Normans were great churchmen, and kings, nobles, and even lesser lords built abbeys and churches. In Cheshire, Anglian and later crosses are among the remains which prove the existence of earlier Christian communities — indeed, Christianity in Cheshire goes back to the early Celtic Church and almost certainly to the Roman period. Few pre-Norman evidences have, unfortunately, survived in Cheshire churches, but the great crosses at Sandbach are the finest in this part of Britain. They are of Mercian type, dated about A.D. 800, and have been re-erected in the market place.

In the later Dark Ages, there were a number of religious communities in Britain, and the earliest house in Cheshire was founded on the site of the present cathedral church of Chester. There the church of Saints Peter and Paul was enlarged by Ethelfleda, the Lady of the Mercians, to become a college of secular canons and it was re-dedicated to St. Werburgh, daughter of King Wulfhere of Mercia whose body had been re-buried there in 875. In 1093, a Benedictine abbey of St. Werburgh was founded by Earl Hugh on the same site, and the building of it, which continued until the sixteenth century, produced the great church and conventual portions so wonderfully preserved as to be one of the great glories of Cheshire.

Birkenhead Priory, of which there are still ruined remains, was another house of Benedictine or 'black monks'. It was founded in the twelfth century and there is Norman work in the west doorway of the restored chapter house, but most of its buildings were dismantled by Cromwellians during the Civil Wars. Cistercians or 'white monks' were at Combermere before the middle of the twelfth century, and much later, in 1277, Edward I founded and built the great Cistercian house of Vale Royal. Stone from Eddisbury, oaks from the Cheshire forests, lead from Flintshire, and nails from Newcastle under Lyme went to its making, and the community of Darnhall moved in leaving Darnhall as a grange. In addition, there were Augustinian canons under their prior at Norton, Cistercians at Stanlow, later attached as a cell to Whalley in Lancashire, and a Benedictine nunnery in Chester. Very different were the friaries or mendicant houses of Chester, whose inmates were vowed to poverty and who, as a result, were generally better loved by the people than were the monastic orders.

Many of the abbots lived in state as great as that of the nobles. The abbeys owned large and scattered estates, those of St. Werburgh's being in over seventy places not only in Cheshire but in other English counties and in North Wales. Much of Chester was owned by St. Werburgh's and much property in Nantwich by Combermere. As landowners, the abbeys were for the most part progressive, extending cultivation, as did the abbot of Vale Royal in Delamere Forest's fringe, and improving the breeds and numbers of farm animals. When the Reformation brought the separation of the Church of England from papal oversight, the wealth of the religious houses tempted the Crown. Many of the communities had shrunk by the early sixteenth century, and some had become lax— yet another cause of the Dissolution of the monasteries which was carried out between 1536 and 1540. Norton Abbey was one of the first to be dissolved, not without protest and

4. Chester, 1829.

5. Lower Bridge Street, Chester, 1829.

6. Gawsworth: The Parish Church and the Pool.

7. The Porch of Chester Cathedral

8. St. John's Church, Chester, believed to have been the eleventh-century cathedral.

9. Prestbury Norman Chapel: Norman doorway.

10. Welsh Row, Nantwich, looking towards the Parish Church.

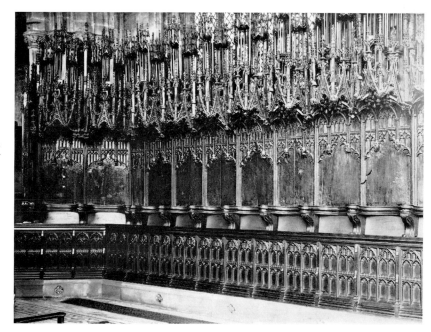

11. Nantwich Parish Church: the Choir Stalls.

12. Bramall Hall.

13. Crewe Hall, a seventeenth-century mansion partly rebuilt.

trouble, probably in 1536. Combermere went in 1538, and became the home of the Cottons including Sir Stapleton, the first Lord Delamere. It was probably in the following year that Vale Royal followed suit, to be bought later by Sir Thomas Holcroft who carried out its dissolution. Now it has disappeared utterly to be replaced by a later house.

St. Werburgh's alone had a different fate, becoming the cathedral church of the Tudor diocese of Chester which was created in 1541 and was endowed with all the rich lands and incomes of the Benedictine house as well as with some which had belonged to Vale Royal, Birkenhead, and St. Mary's nunnery. The new diocese was even larger than the old Norman county but as new sees have been created, it has been cut down to something very similar to the present Cheshire.

Directly and indirectly, the religious houses affected the lives of the ordinary people—townsmen and peasants—but the parish priest and the parish church were much closer to them. To the parish church they went not only to worship on Sundays, but for the feast days, for their own marriages, baptisms, and burials. In the towns, especially Chester, miracle and mystery plays had become popular by the fourteenth century. The parish priests, especially the poorer ones, were generally loved and played a close part in everyday life in town and village. The church was closely linked with markets and fairs, often held in or just outside the church yard. In the towns, the merchant and craft guilds contributed to the income of the church, some building or restoring from their own ample funds, as was the case in the beautiful collegiate church of Nantwich.

In Cheshire the parishes are large and consist, not as in the south of England of one or in a few cases of two or three, but of a great cluster of dependent townships. Even in the early nineteenth century Great Budworth had the second largest number in England, 35, and Prestbury was third with 32, though actually larger in area than Great Budworth. Malpas had 24, Runcorn 19, Wybunbury 18, and Acton (the parish church of Nantwich until the late seventeenth century) 17. Only in west Cheshire and in a few parishes of later origin elsewhere in the county, are small parishes to be found. The parish churches are together the greatest architectural heritage of Cheshire. They date from many periods, but possibly the finest work was that of the late fourteenth and the fifteenth centuries when there was a spate of church building, perhaps in thankfulness for recovery from the Black Death or because death had turned men's minds again to God.

The churches also have an intimate story to tell of the lives of the people and of the events which have taken place in their parishes. Nave and choir, windows and roofs, pulpits and screens, tombs and memorials, towers and doorways, stalls and pews, fonts and chests, and not least church records can be interpreted in relation to the people who created them, and especially rich are the evidences of the Middle Ages in the stone and some of the wood-work of parish churches. Outside, yews were grown for Cheshire bowmen. There were lychgates through which to carry the dead. Stocks were typically placed outside the churchyard wall, and schools built in or near the churchyard where the parish priest was often the teacher too. Malpas, Tarvin, Astbury, Barthomley, Bunbury and Great Budworth churches are almost cathedrals in size: but, large or small, each has a story to tell.

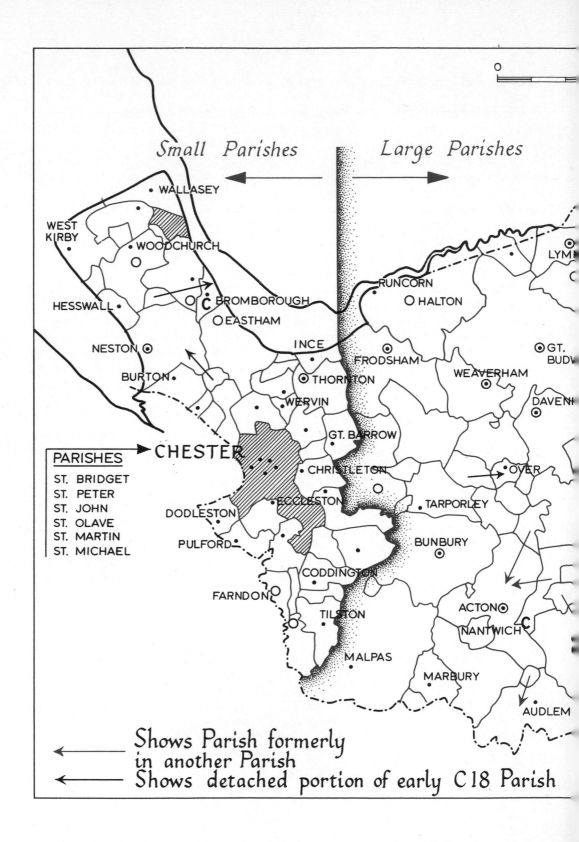

Small Parishes ← → *Large Parishes*

WALLASEY

WEST KIRBY
WOODCHURCH

HESSWALL
BROMBOROUGH
EASTHAM

NESTON
INCE

BURTON

RUNCORN
HALTON

FRODSHAM
THORNTON
WERVIN

WEAVERHAM

GT. BUDW

DAVENI

LYM

CHESTER

GT. BARROW

CHRISTLETON

OVER

PARISHES
ST. BRIDGET
ST. PETER
ST. JOHN
ST. OLAVE
ST. MARTIN
ST. MICHAEL

DODLESTON
ECCLESTON

TARPORLEY

BUNBURY

PULFORD

CODDINGTON

FARNDON

TILSTON

ACTON
NANTWICH

MALPAS

MARBURY

AUDLEM

← ——— Shows Parish formerly in another Parish
← ——— Shows detached portion of early C18 Parish

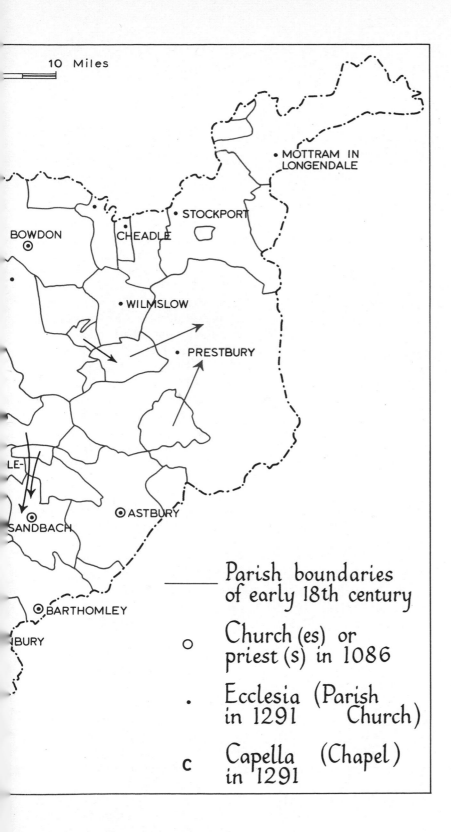

10 Miles

• MOTTRAM IN
LONGENDALE

• STOCKPORT

BOWDON
◉

CHEADLE

• WILMSLOW

• PRESTBURY

LE-

SANDBACH
◉

◉ ASTBURY

◉ BARTHOMLEY

BURY

Parish boundaries
of early 18th century

o   Church (es) or
priest (s) in 1086

.   Ecclesia (Parish
in 1291   Church)

c   Capella (Chapel)
in 1291

CHESHIRE

X

Life in Tudor and Stuart Cheshire

England entered on a period of renewed prosperity with the accession of Henry Tudor, a Welsh speaking Welshman, and his son, Henry VIII, set the seal on the improving relations between Wales and England by the Acts of Union of 1536 and 1542. This made both countries part of a single kingdom and divided that part of Wales not shired in 1284 into six new counties. As Denbighshire was one of these, the last portion of Cheshire's western boundary became fixed, and the marcher lordships came to an end. From 1536, all Cheshire and Welsh justices were appointed by the Crown, and in 1543 Cheshire was represented for the first time at Westminster. The county was at last part of the English realm, though certain features of palatinate organization were retained for some time.

Population recovered from the ravages of the Black Death, again reaching and probably exceeding the total of about 4,000,000 which is estimated to have been the population of England in the early fourteenth century. Agriculture improved, industry and trade expanded, and market towns and ports grew and flourished. Chester, a county town and port, far exceeded all other towns in Cheshire in size and wealth, and remained the largest town in the county until the industrial period. It had the biggest markets, and its numerous manufactures included a variety of cloths and yarns, farm implements and building materials. In the rest of Cheshire, small country towns, many of them with defensive functions, had grown up after the Conquest, but the main boost had been given in the thirteenth century by the creation of boroughs and the conferring of market charters by the earl and the barons. Congleton, Over, Altrincham, Knutsford, and Tarporley boroughs were all chartered at that time, and Macclesfield and Frodsham were founded as dominial boroughs on lands belonging to Earl Ranulf III. Stockport, Halton, Malpas, and the three salt wiches—Nantwich, Northwich, and Middlewich—grew from the early Middle Ages, the last three as dominial salt towns. A curious feature was that six of these towns remained until a late date in the parish of a neighbouring village—Altrincham in Bowdon, Macclesfield in Prestbury, Congleton in Astbury, Knutsford in Rostherne, Halton in Runcorn (the latter eventually outgrowing the ancient borough), and Nantwich in Acton.

The manorial pattern of life did not apply in the boroughs which, in the Middle Ages were governed by the powerful merchant and craft guilds. It was they who built the guild halls some of which later became town halls, and who richly endowed churches and charities. Market tolls brought considerable wealth and market charters were greatly in demand, conferred in the early period not only by the Crown but by the nobility, the bishops and the heads of religious houses. Many markets must have been in existence long before the date of the earliest known charters and for some, as in the case of the three salt wiches, no early charter has survived. Even villages and hamlets might be fortunate enough to acquire a market, for example Aldford and Nether Alderley (both about 1253) and Burton in Wirral (1298). Hardly any markets were chartered in Cheshire in the Tudor and Stuart periods, but Sandbach probably replaced an ancient market at Brereton in 1578, and Tarvin was granted a market in the seventeenth century which died out before 1800. Cheshire has few old market halls, but many historic market places, some in open spaces, others in narrow streets. There might be separate markets for different goods, like the Oat Market and the Swine Market in Nantwich in streets which were paved with leather from Nantwich's tanneries until the late nineteenth century. The Tudor period saw the beginning of what we should now call the central business district, as different crafts and trades took over quarters near the main market place. Booths began to open for retail trade between market days, and inns multiplied to provide for those who came in to buy and sell.

The town plan and old street names are of the greatest interest and use in tracing the functions and character of early towns. The centre of the old towns in usually traceable by the name High Street and by the Market Place or Market Street. The major roads into the town converge near these and the central town plan spreads out from them. If the town lay near a river as did Nantwich and Congleton, Stockport and Macclesfield, a Mill Street led down to the mill which was a feature of town as well as village. In Chester, Stockport and Macclesfield, some of the main streets took the Scandinavian name 'gate' as in Eastgate, Northgate, and Watergate (Chester), Millgate, Churchgate and Petersgate (Stockport), and Wallgate, Chestergate, and Jordangate (Macclesfield). Welsh Row and Welchman's Lane, Nantwich, were so named because of the Welsh drovers whose cattle were driven in on the hoof and who took back salt with which to preserve meat for the winter months when the herds were thinned. The church played a major role in both town and country and a Church Street was to be found in many places and, in Nantwich, a Hospital Street named from a medieval hospital, one of many such as were provided for lepers and other sick by religious orders. The castle and walls were the source of a number of Castle Streets, as in Northwich, and Le Wallgate (Macclesfield). A guild hall, a moot hall, a religious house, a bakehouse, and a market cross or perhaps a market hall were other features of the pre-industrial town, and as trades multiplied, workshops sprang up. In Tudor times, veritable warrens of lanes and alleys crowded with workplaces or with the dwellings of the poor were added to the simpler plan of the medieval town. But they still remained small with the exception of Chester with populations numbering only hundreds in the Middle Ages and perhaps one to two or three thousand at most by the end of the seventeenth century.

Most trades used only simple processes, but their variety was considerable by Stuart and Jacobean times. For instance, in Congleton in 1668 there were skinners, tanners, leather workers, mercers, drapers, silk weavers (in Silk Street), smiths, coopers, chandlers, curriers, bell founders, and a salter. Entertainment was provided from time to time by strolling players and musicians, by the local people taking part in wakes and miracle plays, and by such crude sports as bear baiting and cock fighting. But the period was also notable for the increased interest in education and the multiplication of schools including grammar schools, especially in the seventeenth century. Some of these old schools even go back in foundation to the later Middle Ages and they were to be found in both town and country, a position near to the church being common, as in Tarvin, Bunbury, and Nantwich, and not a few survive to this day. The subjects taught were limited—classical languages, French, Hebrew, mathematics and writing being among the most usual—and there was rarely more than one master, but the effects of the Renaissance and the Reformation were reflected in the increasing demand for schooling, and provided one more proof that the old order was changing and a new age was heralded.

Although feudalism was dying, rural society still remained markedly hierarchical descending from squire, parson, and the larger farmers to lesser farmers and cottagers, with a sprinkling of craftsmen, millers and those engaged in trade. In Cheshire, the

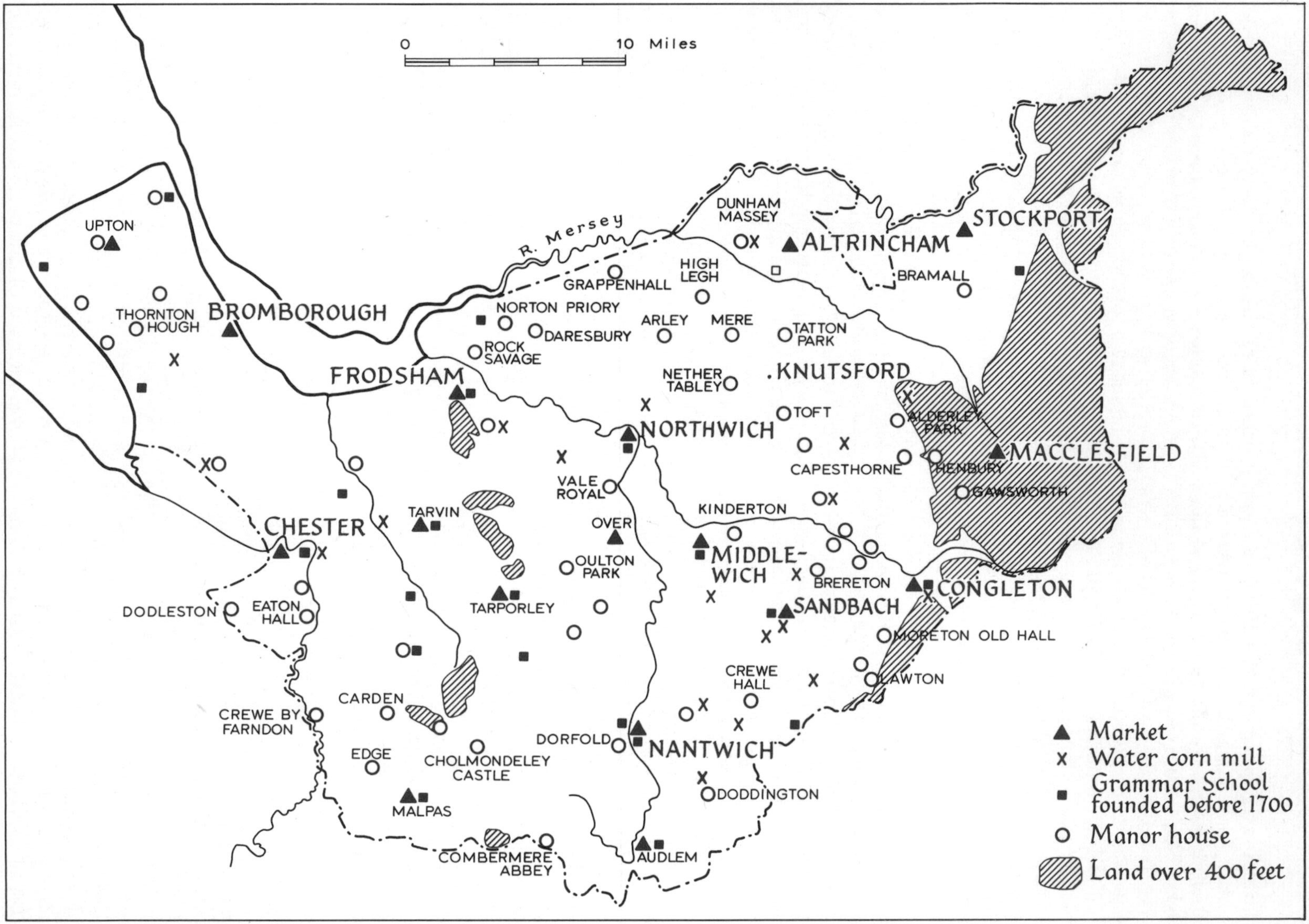

8. TUDOR AND STUART CHESHIRE

Legend:
- Market (▲)
- Water corn mill (×)
- Grammar School founded before 1700 (■)
- Manor house (○)
- Land over 400 feet (hatched)

Place names on map:
STOCKPORT, MACCLESSFIELD, CONGLETON, ALTRINCHAM, BRAMALL, KNUTSFORD, DUNHAM MASSEY, HIGH LEGH, MERE, TATTON PARK, ALDERLEY PARK, PRESTBURY, GAWSWORTH, MORETON OLD HALL, LAWTON, CAPESTHORNE, TOFT, NETHER TABLEY, NORTHWICH, KINDERTON, MIDDLE-WICH, BRERETON, SANDBACH, CREWE HALL, NANTWICH, DODDINGTON, ARLEY, GRAPPENHALL, NORTON PRIORY, DARESBURY, ROCK SAVAGE, FRODSHAM, VALE ROYAL, OVER, OULTON PARK, TARPORLEY, DORFOLD, CHOLMONDELEY CASTLE, AUDLEM, COMBERMERE ABBEY, TARVIN, CARDEN, EDGE, MALPAS, BROMBOROUGH, CHESTER, EATON HALL, CREWE BY FARNDON, DODLESTON, THORNTON, HOUGH, UPTON

R. Mersey

10 Miles

42

characteristic pattern was of parochial villages surrounded by the hamlets and scattered farms of their dependent townships, and it was probably in this period that the villages experienced the first marked growth since the tragic shrinkage of the fourteenth century. New and improved cottages and houses were built, and it was the heyday of the small manor house nowhere more important than in Cheshire, 'the seedplot of gentility'. Ample timber was still available and, although stone was used in the Pennines and where suitable New Red Sandstones emerged, over the greater part of the county, it was the carpenters and sawyers who built the half-timbered or frame houses which are the glory of Cheshire to this day. This method of building was known as 'timber nogging'. Among the most beautiful frame houses in Britain are the three-storied Moreton Old Hall and the Crown Hotel, Nantwich. Other outstanding examples of half-timbered manor houses are Bramall Hall and Gawsworth Old Hall and, among merchants' houses, Churche's Mansion, Nantwich.

In 1580, some of the families mentioned in the Domesday Book were still lords of the manors in Cheshire, many spreading through collateral branches. For instance, the Leghs of High Legh who trace their ancestry to Richard Earl of Cornwall and brother of Henry III and to Hywel Dda and other Welsh princes, held nine manorial seats, and the Masseys were similarly holders of another nine. Dod of Edge claims an ancestry going back to before the Norman Conquest, and other ancient families are the Davenports, the Breretons, the Stanleys and the Mainwarings. Many were linked by marriage and combined their names (the Bromley-Davenports and the Grey-Egertons), some changed their surnames, and many died out. The Civil Wars and the Restoration saw further changes and in west Cheshire, especially in the Dee valley, numbers of manor houses dropped to the status of large farmhouses from that time.

XI

The Civil Wars in Cheshire

After two hundred years of peace Cheshire was ill prepared for the conflicts which broke out in 1643. The dissension between King and Parliament was a major turning point in the constitutional history of this country for it was essentially a struggle for supreme power, and the Parliamentary victory meant the end of the absolute power of the monarchy even after the Restoration. It was more than a political issue, however, for it was inextricably linked with religious questions—broadly the growing differences between Episcopacy and Presbyterianism on the one hand and Independence and Puritanism on the other. In the seventeenth century it meant that virtually everyone took sides and G. M. Trevelyan has described the resulting civil wars as 'the most terrible storm in English history'.

There was no clear geographical division between Royalist (or Cavalier) and Parliamentary (or Roundhead) sympathisers for both were represented in every county, every town, and many a village. But on the whole, Wales and south-western England, the extreme North and the north-east supported the King, while London, south-eastern England, and the eastern counties as far north as the Humber were Parliamentarian. So too were the Midlands, the woollen manufacturing districts of West Yorkshire and south-east Lancashire, and most of Cheshire. But there was a division between Royalist west Cheshire based on Chester and central and east Cheshire which were predominantly Parliamentarian and this became the basis of the major strategy and much of the course of the war in the county. Chester was a Royalist stronghold throughout the years 1643–6. From the Royalist point of view it

had the advantage of being on the flanks of Royalist Wales, a major road centre commanding the North Wales coast road and the road south down the Welsh Borderland, the largest town in Cheshire and strongly protected by its walls and castle. In addition, although the Dee at Chester was by then heavily silted, the port of Chester stretched down the estuary and its outports were vital in bringing in food and supplies and reinforcements from Wales and Ireland. It became even more important as the Parliamentarians' hold on sea communications tightened. Twenty-three miles away, the much smaller town of Nantwich—but still the second in size in Cheshire—was the Parliamentarian centre. It too was a major road centre, controlling the routes from London to north-western England and to North Wales north of the Midland Gate, but it was extremely difficult to defend. Stockport, Macclesfield and, rather less important, Middlewich and Northwich were also Parliamentarian towns.

Military service, which was implicit under the feudal system, had died a natural death during the peaceful reigns of the Tudors and the early Stuarts, and both sides had to assemble an army hastily and give such sketchy training as was possible in the time. The first campaigns were fought by raggedly disciplined and ill-equipped men and it was not until the formation of the New Model Army later in the war that the tide turned for the Roundheads. At the beginning, both sides depended on the nobles and on local gentry to raise soldiery from their own estates. In Cheshire, the aristocracy were on the whole Royalist—the Grosvenors, the Stanleys, the Lords Cholmondeley, Brereton, and Rivers. The lesser gentry were divided—Sir

Edward Fytton, Legh of Adlington, Tatton of Wythenshawe, and the Roman Catholic Masseys, Hockenhulls and Pooles were for the King as were also many of the great merchant families. For the Parliamentarians were Sir William Brereton of Handforth, one of the principal commanders in Cheshire, Sir George Booth of Dunham, Brooks of Norton, Wilbraham of Woodhey, various branches of the Mainwarings, Delves of Doddington, and most families eminent in the law.

There were three main phases in the Cheshire conflict: the Nantwich phase 1643–4, the Chester phase 1644–6, and the third and, for Cheshire, the least important one, in which the county was rarely the scene of active fighting (1649–51).

In January 1643, Sir William Brereton rode from the Pennine hills down into Congleton with some three hundred men at arms and, a day later on 28 January after a skirmish with the Royalists, he took over Nantwich. In the absence of walls, he threw up earthen defences, garrisoned the town and made it the key point in Parliamentarian strategy in Cheshire east of the Dee valley. In answer, the Royalists already established in Chester, strengthened the defences of the Dee bridges at Farndon, Bangor, and Overton. Brereton took Middlewich for the Roundheads in March and was soon afterwards proclaimed the commander of all their forces in Cheshire. One of his chief tasks was to maintain the lines of communication with Stockport and Manchester to the north and with the Midlands and London beyond the Midland Gate. The royal stronghold of Beeston Castle on its precipitous sandstone rock, guarding the main road to North Wales through the Beeston Gap, was captured by the Parliamentarians, as were the Mersey bridges, and by the autumn of 1643, the Parliamentarian armies were more successful in Cheshire than anywhere else in the country where the Royalists were carrying all before them.

In November, they embarrassed the Royalists in Chester by launching an en-circling movement which extended from Farndon to Holt, round to Hawarden and the North Wales coast road, so that they cut off the land road by which supplies were taken into Chester. But it proved of only temporary use, for 4,000 Royalist infantry were landed at Mostyn and 1,000 cavalry brought up from Oxford, easily breaking through the Roundheads' overstretched lines. Worse was to follow for the Parliamentarians for these forces moved south-east to besiege Nantwich and from November until January 1644 the town was beleaguered. Beeston Castle was won back by the Royalists; their troops stationed at points encircling the little town, and the townsfolk harried constantly. Near Middlewich, Brereton was defeated with the loss of 500 men when he attempted to move south from Kinderton Hall, and it was Sir Thomas Fairfax who moved in next, marching from Lincolnshire via Stafford and Newcastle under Lyme. But he was diverted by Royalist sallies and only after reinforcements were brought in from Manchester and the Scottish Border was the issue settled. The battle of Nantwich was fought on 25 January 1644 and was a major victory for the Parliamentarians who also captured the surrounding garrisons and took 1,500 captive.

An improvement in Royalist fortunes occurred in May of that year when that dashing young Prince Rupert came into Cheshire from Shrewsbury via Audlem and encamped his army on Rudheath, Knutsford Heath, and Bowdon Downs. He cut across Parliamentarian lines at Stockport and moved into south Lancashire to be joined at Liverpool by Byron bringing large numbers of horse and foot from Chester. For a time all Lancashire apart from the garrisons at Manchester and Warrington appeared to be in their hands, and in Cheshire only Nantwich and the small garrison at Northwich remained to the Parliamentarians. There was confusion as regards tactics and also because there were too many leaders in both Lancashire and Cheshire, but eventually

9. THE CIVIL WARS

Parliament's forces captured Oswestry and then Sir William Brereton marched across the Pennines. He helped to rout the Royalist forces led by Prince Rupert, at Marston Moor, near York, on 2 July 1644, after which Royalist armies were in retreat both in Lancashire and along the Welsh Border.

Late that year, the siege of Chester was mounted by Brereton at the head of troops from Cheshire and Staffordshire together with some Irish. By this time, the discipline, equipment and training of Parliamentarian forces had everywhere improved. (Oliver Cromwell's New Model Army was already foreshadowed, and was in being in 1645.) Chester, however, unlike Nantwich, was strongly defended by its high medieval walls and gates. It still had long communication lines by land and sea, considerable resources of food and equipment, and a large population. Brereton placed his troops at various points around the city but the siege was long and the fighting bitter. The occupants burnt many of the houses in the eastern suburbs as part of a scorched earth policy, and there was similar destruction along Eastgate and Watergate.

On 24 September the Royalist armies were soundly beaten at the battle of Rowton Moor two miles to the south-east of the city, and from the Phoenix Tower, now more usually called King Charles' Tower, the King watched the return of his broken army. Despite this defeat, the city still held out, but by January the people and the troops alike within the walls were suffering acutely from exhaustion and starvation and, at last, on 3 February 1646 the city surrendered.

After three years, hostilities were over but in many ways the peace was a sad and hollow one. Crops had been trampled or commandeered year after year for fighting men, cattle seized, and almost every horse taken for the cavalry. Supplies of all kinds including food were short and the county was war weary but, strangely enough, there was little bitterness between those who so recently had fought on opposite sides. After the execution of Charles I in 1649, war broke out again and Cheshire men once more served in the forces, but active war was carried on elsewhere.

A late echo was the Cheshire Rising of 1659, in part religious, and led by George Booth the Younger of Dunham Massey. The entire county fell into his hands and the revolt spread to Lancashire, Staffordshire, and North Wales. Young Sir George was by this time a Royalist and, pursued by forces of the New Model Army, he was captured and imprisoned in the Tower of London. The separate jurisdiction of the County Palatine was suspended as a result of the rising, but Palatine status was restored in 1660 and Sir George released without trial later to act as intermediary between the Lords and the Commons when the question of the recall of Charles II arose. He thus became the chief Cheshire agent of the Restoration of 1660.

XII

Cheshire Agriculture in the Eighteenth and Nineteenth centuries

The change in the economic climate which was heralded in the seventeenth century began to burgeon in the eighteenth century both in the agricultural and manufacturing industries. Causes, progress, and effects were nationwide and far from simple and both the agrarian and industrial aspects of this major economic revolution were closely interlocked. Population is one of the most useful yardsticks by which to measure the success or failure of a changing national economy. Prior to the first Census of Population in 1801, only round estimates are available but using these, it is possible to say that the population of England and Wales after dropping to about 2·5 million after the Black Death rose slowly to about 5 million in 1600 and 5·8 million in 1700. The rate of increase accelerated in the eighteenth century and by 1801 it had risen by almost exactly 50 per cent to 8·89 million. The increased production and prosperity of the early period of the agrarian and industrial revolutions are undoubtedly reflected in these figures. But the full tide of change had yet to come and it was the nineteenth century which saw the fulfilment of the earlier trends. By the end of the century, the population of England and Wales had almost quadrupled, totalling 32·5 million in 1901. The rate of increase naturally varied from very high amounts in the more industrialized counties to very modest ones in the predominantly rural ones. Cheshire lay between the two extremes, but inclined more towards the former. From a population of 191,000 in 1801, the total more than doubled to 420,000 in 1851, and nearly doubled again in the latter half of the century to 816,000 in 1901, an increase for the century rather above the national average but well below that of Lancashire.

Although the salt industry was expanding in mid-Cheshire, and small textile industries and some metal industries were growing up in east Cheshire, the county was overwhelmingly agricultural throughout the eighteenth century and, even after the rapid growth of industry and of urban population in the nineteenth century, agriculture remained of great importance in the economy. Like the northern counties in general, its agriculture was less intensive and its land less fully taken up than in the south of England and Henry Holland writing in 1808 described it as follows: 'The general appearance of Cheshire is that of an extended plain, thickly covered with wood; so that from some points the whole country resembles one vast and continued forest . . . . From Macclesfield, in a north-westerly direction, the surface is irregular and hilly. . .'. Its rainfall is under 30 inches per annum except for the north and north-east of the county which is out of the rain shadow of the Welsh uplands but, although rainfall is moderate, its cool northerly position and the predominance of glacial clays over wide stretches of the plain encourage the growth of woodland and, when cleared, give a rich sward well suited to dairying.

Agriculturally, it had never been in the van of progress and the advances in agricultural practice introduced by such pioneers as Jethro Tull, Robert Bakewell, Arthur Young and Coke of Holkham were not adopted quickly in Cheshire, even if they were applicable (and some were not so) in a county where corn growing was limited by the climate and became less popular as markets

14. The Anderton Lift linking the Weaver Navigation with the Trent and Mersey Canal.

15. Bonewaldesthorne's Tower at the north-west corner of Chester city walls. The Water Tower is seen below it on the right.

Engraved by I.Walker from an Original Drawing by H. Orme.

Published May 1 1797 by I. Walker, No Rosoman Street, London.

16. Stockport in 1680.

17. Stockport Market Place *circa* 1810.

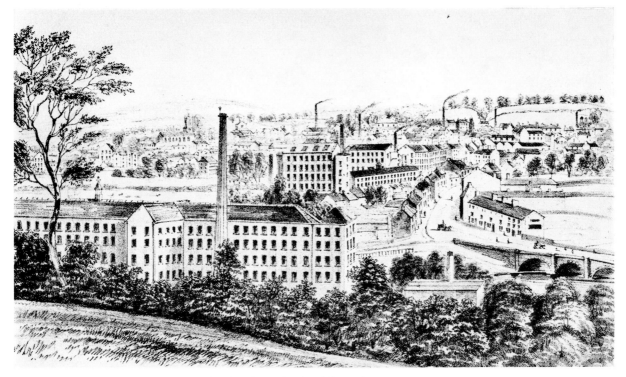

18. Congleton in the eighteenth century.

19. Northwich, subsidence near the Dane Bridge as a result of salt extraction.

20. Birkenhead: East and West Floats and docks, and old grid-plan town centre.

21. Port Sunlight: houses in the garden village.

and transport facilities improved. There were other factors also which differentiated Cheshire from the south and south-east of England. It was not, on the whole, an area of large farms, very few being as big as 500 acres and many totalling only 10–30 acres, small holdings practising a mixed economy. There were, of course a number of large estates such as the Tollemache estate in mid-Cheshire and the Derby estates in the east and they played a part in the changing conditions of tenure in the eighteenth and nineteenth centuries, but even in 1851 there were only eleven farms in the county of over 500 acres and on half the 6,663 farm holdings no labour was employed. Enclosure which, according to the Enclosure Awards in the Cheshire Record Office, covered the period 1767 to 1898, was principally of open common land, not of open arable fields except in very small acreages, for open field enclosure had been piecemeal and gradual in Cheshire. In most Cheshire enclosures of the common, allotments were made for the former commoners, and numerous small-holdings arose, typically with a cottage on an acre or two of land sufficient to produce a few crops and to support a cow, a pig or two, and some fowls. The social boundary between farmer and farm labourer was very blurred.

The bias toward animal farming and towards dairying in particular, increased as trade in agricultural produce moved more freely and especially when the repeal of the Corn Laws in 1846 allowed corn prices to fall and foreign wheat to come in. Cheshire farms grew oats, potatoes and hay for preference, and some wheat for home use. In the seventeenth century, cheese, salt beef, and bacon had been the main agricultural exports. In the eighteenth century, cheese continued to be the main agricultural product and in the 1790s Wedge made a similar observation but also noted the increase in tillage with corn, especially oats, and some mixed crops predominating. In 1808, Holland stressed the fact that wheat, oats, and

potatoes were the principal crops and that others, though less common, were barley, turnips, cabbages, kohl rabi, beans, peas, carrots, onions, buckwheat, and rye. Crop management on the whole was poor and there were few arable farms except on the sands east of Delamere which specialized in corn and potatoes with some sheep. Particular attention was paid to meadows and pastures, and for that reason there was growing interest in clover, sainfoin, and grasses, the results being so good that turnip growing was rare until the 1840s when it began to be more widely used in the rotation. Green fodder with vetches and rye, the ox cabbage which gave a high yield from 1800, and hay were raised in increasing amounts and green crops replaced fallowing. Where rotation was practised, it was usual to interpolate a few years of leys, but the prejudice towards permanent pasture remained strong. An important result of the increased output of hay and green fodder was the abandonment of the ancient practice of thinning the herds drastically in the autumn. This meant that winter feed was possible and thus the milk yield could be maintained throughout the year—particularly useful in view of the growing urban population. The towns also demanded large quantities of potatoes and increasing amounts of other vegetables. These began to be the specialized output of the north Cheshire farms where there are extensive patches of sands and sandy loams, and where the town populations were growing with considerable rapidity especially from the mid-nineteenth century.

Animal husbandry remained the mainstay of Cheshire farms in the plain south of the Mersey belt, becoming more and more a specialization as the nineteenth century saw the decline of the more backward, traditional type of farming and as the market widened for dairy produce. Although selective breeding was rare and herds averaged only from 10 to 60 head of cattle, the milk yield was exceptionally high from a total of up to 100,000 dairy cows in the county. Bullocks were also fattened for the market, and horses were kept in numbers for ploughing, riding, and draught as well as for the hunt. The large coarse bacon pig was reared and until the nineteenth century the old practice was followed of feeding them in the woods and on the commons, but the enclosure movement and the increased importance of dairying brought them into farm sties where, fed on skim milk, whey, and vegetable refuse, they formed the ideal complement of the dairy and mixed crop farms and smallholdings. Sheep were kept mainly on the Pennine moors, on the sandier soils of the plain, or on the stubble on corn-growing farms, and by the 1840s there were probably some 65,000 sheep in the county. Wool was the principal interest of the sheep farmer who sold his wool crop to clothiers in the small woollen centres which were to be found in north-east Cheshire and adjoining areas of the Pennines. Again, breeding was rarely pure, but early in the nineteenth century merino rams were introduced to improve the wool.

Enclosure began long before the first parliamentary awards in Cheshire where, apart from Frodsham, no complete system of open arable fields remained by 1767. The open fields had never had the size and regularity of those of the south Midlands and south of England, but had consisted more typically of a number of small fields. Even where a three-year system had been worked, as at Tarvin and Wybunbury and doubtless in many other places, their irregular and scattered character lent itself to early exchange, compacting and enclosure. But the relatively moderate density of the rural population meant that there was considerable common left in the form of moorland, heath, peat moss, and even of potentially good farming land. Parliamentary enclosure accounted for the greater part of this between the mideighteenth and the mid-nineteenth century. Some of the commons were already encroached on by industrial concerns, as in the Macclesfield area, and by squatters. But

large acreages went in allotments of very varying size to smallholders and farmers, even though the squires kept some for themselves to add to demesne land. The result was a spate of building and the small brick cottages and the large, flat-fronted, three-storeyed farmhouses of this phase can be traced in innumerable townships over the Cheshire Plain, and stone editions of these on the eastern moorlands. Many of the lesser holders were part-time labourers and in the depression years following 1875 were in dire economic straits. Some sought to work in the towns, many emigrated, and their sparse acres were absorbed into neighbouring farms. Many of these scattered cottages with their tiny paddocks still survive, however, and are a distinctive feature of the settlement pattern.

Advancing methods in agricultural practice were comparatively slow to reach northwestern England, but the increasing population of industrial towns in Lancashire and on its borders, and the food shortage due to the Napoleonic Wars stimulated production and favoured new methods in Cheshire about the turn of the century. Enclosure of moor, peat moss, and of clayey areas demanded drainage, and tile drains were used from about 1830. This drew attention to waterlogged pastures and the soil was lightened by ploughing up, mixing in straw stubble, liming, and draining. Ridge and furrow ploughing, especially during the food shortage period of the Napoleonic Wars, also helped and was employed until about 1845. This narrow ridge and furrow is widely traceable in Cheshire pastures to this day. Main ditches were actually supervised by constables or burleymen and offenders brought up before the court leet.

Manuring was another of the improvements adopted comparatively readily in Cheshire. Farm manure was plentiful, and was used together with night soil by the growing number of market gardeners as the century advanced. Guano and nitrate of soda were used in the 1840s but were found to encourage too rank a herbage. What was most needed on the clays was calcium in one form or another and it was increasingly added in the form of lime from Derbyshire and bone meal. The latter proved especially effective and, although expensive, its effect was lasting. Bone mills were set up at a number of places, and the cheese and milk yield soared.

Many of the agricultural implements invented at this period were of little interest to Cheshire farmers, but turnip cutters, the winnowing machine and the grinder were being employed by 1800. Soon afterwards, the newly invented 'tedder' or haymaking machine was adopted on the larger farms, and a few with a fair tillage acreage used the threshing machine. Most of the harvest-ing continued to be done by hand, but iron replaced wood where possible and implements were valuable.

The improvement in the roads brought definite benefit to the farmers and it was, indeed, the Board of Agriculture which was pressing many of the improvements. As surfaces improved, more farm wagons were bought both for the farm and to take produce to market. A great amount of cheese was shipped by canal to all parts of the country, but the turnpike roads encouraged farmers to do their own transporting to nearer markets. The change from subsistence to commercial agriculture was achieved, and the farmer took his place as an important agent in forwarding the economic revolution.

XIII

Waterways and Roads

The position of Cheshire is such that it spans the major routes from London to north-western England and North Wales, and from the south-west to the north-west of England, as well as lying midway along the western sea routes. This has been reflected through the ages in the concentration of land and sea-routes on Chester, in the focal position of Nantwich as a road centre north of the Midland Gate, and in the centuries-old use of the Mersey crossing between Wilderspool and Warrington. With the expansion of industry, trade, and shipping in the seventeenth century, these factors gave Cheshire an enhanced importance in relation to the growing network of national and local communications by land and sea. In the eighteenth century, Cheshire waterways became linked up with the national system of navigations and canals which were to be so significant in the early phase of the Industrial Revolution. Prior to the railway era, the story falls into three parts: the ports and sea trade of the Dee and Mersey estuaries, the turnpike roads, and the inland waterways.

From prehistoric times, the Dee estuary had been used in trade across the waters of the Irish Sea. With the coming of the Romans, ships came here from many parts of the Empire as well as from the coasts of Britain and, when the Normans adopted Chester as the seat and administrative centre of the earldom and county of Chester, the port entered on a period of major prosperity, becoming the head port of a stretch of coastline extending from the Lleyn Peninsula to north Lancashire. When King John dispatched troops to Ireland from Chester, the permanent organization of the port was in being with its three principal officers—the customer, comptroller, and searcher—resident in the city. Together with the port of Bristol, it controlled the shipping and seaborne trade of the entire west coast of England, while Liverpool, one of its 'creeks', was a minor trading centre on the far less important estuary of the Mersey. At the time of the Roman occupation, the Roodee (now Chester race course) was the site of the estuary head with a bottom level some 15 inches below the present surface, and ships sailed in to tie up at the harbour wall behind it. But the smothering sands began their work and from about 1400, with silting a definite menace, some vessels unloaded at the Hyle Lake (Hoylake). Other outports along the estuarine shores gradually took over much of the work of the port which, because of the revival of trade with Ireland from 1500, was expanding. Shotwick, Burton, Neston (the Old Quay), Parkgate (the New Quay), and Heswall all filled this role until they in turn became silt-logged—Parkgate only in the 1820s. In the sixteenth century, the Mersey's connections with Ireland were also becoming closer due to the demand for flax to mix with wool by the growing textile industry of south-east Lancashire, and by the time of Elizabeth I the trade of the two estuaries was equal. In 1660, the area of the 'liberties' of the two ports was defined, and in 1671, Liverpool controlled both banks of the Mersey estuary and its trade outstripped that of Chester. Chester continued to be the head port through most of the seventeenth century, its administration extending from Barmouth to the Duddon, but from being one of six named ports in the kingdom in 1558, it had sunk to 36th in order of vessels entering and clearing the port in 1716. In the eighteenth century the triangular trade in slaves and cotton, and the rapid growth of industrial Lancashire brought about the ascendancy of the Mersey, long foreshadowed by the silting of the sister estuary. Chester continued as a relatively minor port, though somewhat restored by the New Cut made in 1754 to straighten the main channel of the river from Chester to the more open waters of the estuary.

Meanwhile, apart from the savage interruption of the Civil Wars, the economy of the county advanced in common with that of the rest of Britain. Except for short stretches immediately above the estuaries of the Dee and the Weaver, Cheshire had no navigable inland waters, and from the Dark Ages onwards trade had of necessity used either the Roman roads or the worn trackways from village to village. By Tudor times, their appalling condition at last caused anxiety, and in 1555 the Highway Act took the task of road maintenance from the manors and gave it to the parishes. The condition of the roads in most parishes worsened. The first turnpike trust was formed in 1663 and magistrates and surveyors were made responsible for repair. Still the effect was negligible but the dawn was heralded, and it was the introduction of coaches which at last brought home both to merchants and to an increasing number of the travelling public that better roads were an urgent necessity. A further proof of the growing interest in road improvement was the publication by John Ogilby of the first complete survey of British roads in his *Britannia* in 1674. Only a few turnpike trusts were formed in the seventeenth and the early eighteenth centuries, but by 1800 most of the inter-parochial roads and the main Roman roads in Cheshire had been turnpiked, including the ancient salters' roads which hinged on the three 'wiches' and by which salt was sent to Wales and the Borderland and most parts of northern and eastern England. The main need was to improve construction and surfacing for most roads were deeply rutted, dust bowls in a dry season, quagmires in a wet. The first important step was taken by General George Wade

who, after the 1715 Rebellion, made 800 miles of smooth-surfaced roads in Scotland. The matter was increasingly urgent. By 1637, the first coach known to run to timetable plied between Birmingham and Holywell via Nantwich and Chester. In 1657, a service began between London and Chester, running three times a week and taking four days for the journey. In 1776, the service was extended to Holyhead and operated daily from Chester and, from 1780, daily from London to Holyhead, while four years later the first mail coach ran on this route replacing the post boys. The London-Holyhead road, entering the county from Newcastle under Lyme at Bridgemere, passed through Nantwich and Chester, making it Cheshire's major road, and contributing considerably to the importance of both towns. By this date, the agrarian and industrial revolutions were well under way. Further, the Act which in 1805 brought Ireland into the United Kingdom had increased still more the need for fast communications between London and Holyhead. In 1810, the first parliamentary committee was appointed to deal with major through routes and the Holyhead road was the first of these. It was surveyed by the great road and canal engineer Thomas Telford, and constructed between 1815 and 1830 along a route which passed through Shrewsbury and Llangollen and no longer through Cheshire.

Road making continued apace, surfaces improving beyond all recognition when from 1826, MacAdam's new methods of construction and surfacing spread to other parts of the country. Most of Cheshire's main highways were turnpiked by 1820. The greater number were old highways, but some new roads were cut, especially near growing industrial centres and the new towns of north Wirral. This was the heyday of the coaching age, the peak activity dating from about 1820, but it was to be short-lived for the railway era was at hand. By 1850, coaching was stone dead and the roads went into decline, used only for local traffic until after the

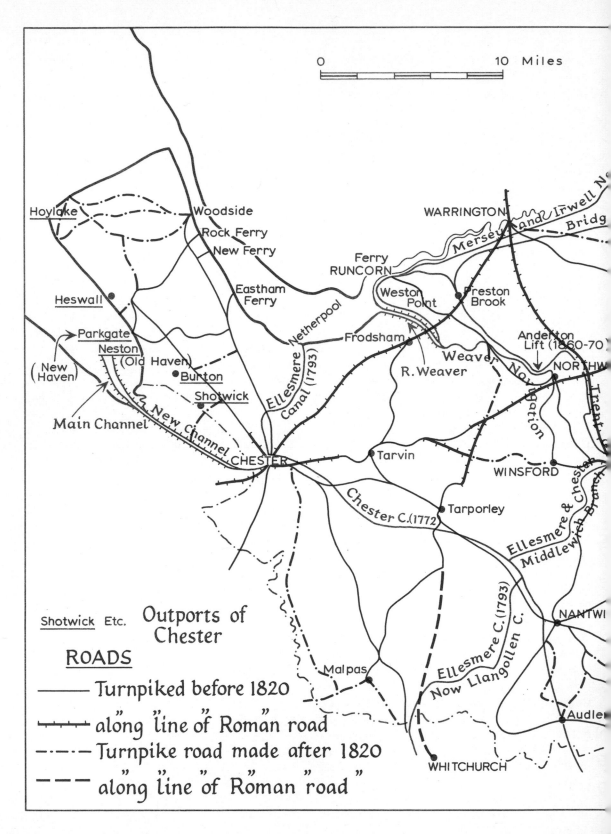

Outports of Chester

Shotwick Etc.

ROADS

—— Turnpiked before 1820

⊢⊢⊢ along "line of Roman road

—·—· Turnpike road made after 1820

– – – " " " " "
along "line of Roman "road" "

Map labels:

0   10 Miles

Hoylake

Woodside

Rock Ferry

New Ferry

Eastham Ferry

WARRINGTON

Mersey and Irwell N.

Brid.

Ferry
RUNCORN

Weston
Point

Preston
Brook

Heswall

Netherpool

Parkgate
Neston
(Old Haven)

(New
Haven)

Burton

Shotwick

Frodsham

R. Weaver

Weaver

Anderton
Lift (1860-70)

NORTHW

Main Channel

New Channel

Ellesmere Canal (1793)

Navigation

Trent

CHESTER

Tarvin

WINSFORD

Ellesmere & Chester

Chester C. (1772)

Tarporley

Middlewich Branch

NANTWI

Ellesmere C. (1793)
Now Llangollen C.

Malpas

Audle

WHITCHURCH

10. TURNPIKE RO

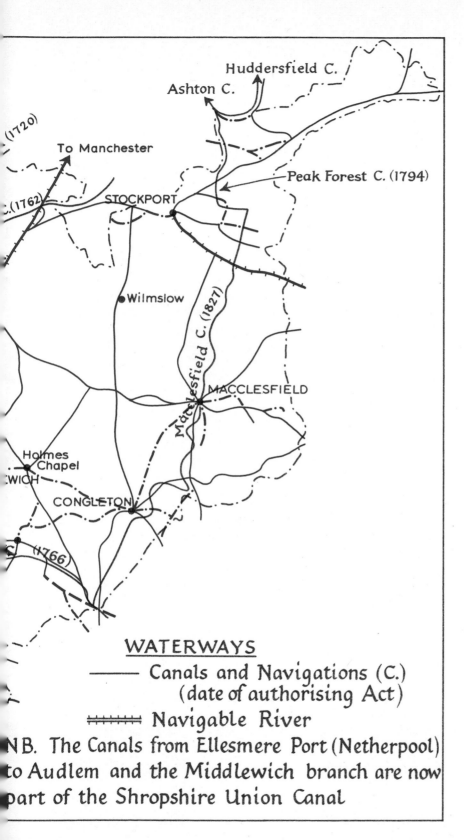

WATERWAYS

────── Canals and Navigations (C.)
            (date of authorising Act)
┼┼┼┼┼┼ Navigable River

N B. The Canals from Ellesmere Port (Netherpool)
to Audlem and the Middlewich branch are now
part of the Shropshire Union Canal

Railway Strike of 1911. The turnpike trusts were finally abolished in 1895, but only in 1937 did the Ministry of Transport assume responsibility for the main trunk roads.

The canal era began in Cheshire with two 'navigations', that is with the straightening and deepening of the lower course of the river Weaver and the Mersey and Irwell Navigation. The date of the Acts for both projects was 1720. In 1759 an Act was passed authorizing the first wholly artificial water-way and this canal—the Bridgewater named after the Duke who floated the scheme—was designed and built by the first of the great canal engineers, James Brindley, and it was opened in 1762. There followed the Acts for the Grand Trunk (now the Trent and Mersey) in 1766, for the Chester Canal 1772, for the Ellesmere and Ashton Canals 1792 and 1793, the Huddersfield 1794, the Peak Forest in the same year, and in the early nineteenth century the Birmingham and Liverpool Junction Canal (1826) and the Macclesfield (1827). Only a very short stretch of the Ashton and Huddersfield Canals lay in Cheshire, and the Mersey and Irwell Navigation has now been superseded by the Manchester Ship Canal (opened in 1894). All the old canals are narrow barge canals but the Weaver Navigation has been constantly improved. For 140 years, it was not connected with the narrow canals but in 1860–70 the Anderton Lift was built near Northwich to enable boats to pass from the Weaver to the Trent and Mersey Canal and vice versa, so from that date all Cheshire's navigable inland waterways became part of the north-western branch of the English canal system which is shaped like an hour glass centred on Birmingham. The aim of the canal planners was, basically, to provide cheap water transport and to link up with the major estuaries of the Mersey, Humber, Severn and Thames and their navigable tributaries and from the main system to send branches to certain other inland places. The northern Cheshire canals served or linked up with the Mersey towns of both Cheshire

and Lancashire and, beyond these, with West Yorkshire. The Weaver Navigation and the Trent and Mersey served both the salt field and the North Staffordshire coalfield. The western canals (the Ellesmere, Chester, and Birmingham and Liverpool Junction, now all part of the Shropshire Union) were the main north-western line of the Birmingham–Mersey link; the more southerly Ellesmere Canal (now the Llangollen Canal) ended at Llantysilio above Llangollen and has carried comparatively little traffic. The Peak Forest and the Macclesfield, among the last to be built were too late to offer very effective competition to the railways once mid-century was passed, but the Macclesfield carried coal, quarried-stone, metal goods, pottery and some textiles in fair quantities until 1914.

Taken as a whole, the canal network combined with sea lanes to make a notable contribution to the development of Cheshire's economy in the eighteenth and early nineteenth centuries. The salt industry and, later, the chemical industry were to benefit particularly and, in the east of the county, the canals afforded cheap if slow transport for the raw materials and finished goods of the rapidly developing textile industry, for engineering, chemicals (such as bleaches and dyestuffs for the silk and cotton mills), and for the vast amounts of building material required in the expanding industrial towns.

Runcorn and, later, Weston became sea, river, and canal ports as a result of the linking up of the Bridgewater Canal and the Weaver Navigation with the Mersey, and the tiny settlement of Netherpool at the northern terminus of the Ellesmere Canal from Chester was later to grow into Ellesmere Port.

The Trent and Mersey, earlier known as the Grand Trunk Canal, was one of the last canals to be planned and engineered by James Brindley, and the first sod was cut by Josiah Wedgwood. Near its northern end are three tunnels, the first in the world to be cut for waterway transport and, just outside the county, Brindley built the narrow 'legging' tunnel at Harecastle through which, for many years, barges were propelled by bargees pushing with their feet against the tunnel roof. A loftier tunnel was built alongside this in 1827 by Thomas Telford.

Unlike the roads, the canals were not entirely overshadowed by the railways and, although they suffered relative decline especially on routes away from the coalfields, their rates for freight of high bulk and low value which could stand slower delivery were so favourable that many continued to play an important part in transport.

They were true heralds of the coming era of large scale industrialization.

XIV

The Railway Age

The first phase of the Industrial Revolution was almost over by the time the next and more effective change took place in the transport revolution—that of the coming of the railways. Wooden wagonways go back as far as the sixteenth century. A stationary steam engine was perfected by James Watt in the 1760s and applied to the driving of textile machinery in the 1780s, but the first high pressure steam engine to run on rails was evolved by Richard Trevithick in 1800 and tried out at Penydarran near Merthyr Tydfil in 1804. Hedley's Puffing Billy ran at Wylam mines in 1813, and twelve years later the Stockton and Darlington railway became the first in the world to open for passenger traffic, with George Stephenson as its engineer. The second was the Liverpool and Manchester in 1830, and Cheshire was soon to follow, its generally level terrain being ideal for the purpose.

The first railway line to be constructed in Cheshire was the Grand Junction (Birmingham to Warrington) which entered the county a few miles south of Crewe. The first railway station at Crewe was opened in 1837 and three years later the Crewe–Chester–Birkenhead line came into operation within a system which, by that date, linked London, Leeds, Lancaster, and Gloucester with the Liverpool–Manchester line. Only ten years later, the greater portion of the national network north-west of the Chester–London line was in being. What was later to be part of the Great Western Railway from Chester down the west of England reached Ruabon in 1846. The important Irish connection via Holyhead and Chester was opened as far as Mold Junction in 1848 and completed in 1849, crossing the Menai Straits by Robert Stephenson's Britannia Tubular Bridge. Chester was then the centre of four railway routes; by 1874, when the Cheshire Lines Railway was completed from Manchester, it was the centre of five; and of six when a line from Northgate station to Hawarden Bridge was added in 1890.

Meantime, with the refusal of Nantwich to house the Grand Junction railway works, Crewe had become not only the seat of the works but the centre of six lines, all of major importance. It was linked with Manchester in 1842, with Stoke-on-Trent in 1848, and with Shrewsbury in 1858. Five years later it was connected via Nantwich with Market Drayton, thus becoming the major railway junction in Cheshire and one of the largest in the country. Stockport was third in importance, mainly as the junction of the Manchester–Crewe line with the 1857 line into Derbyshire via Whaley Bridge, but its other incoming lines were of local significance linking it with the nearby cotton towns. In 1849, east Cheshire acquired a through line from Stoke-on-Trent via Congleton, Macclesfield, and Cheadle Hulme to Manchester, but the final connection between London and Liverpool via Crewe was only made in 1869 when an extension from Weaver Junction crossed the Mersey at Runcorn. Some lesser railways remained to be added in north-east Cheshire and in Wirral but the major part of the Cheshire network was complete by 1875.

The 'railway mania' of the 1840s and 1850s effected a second stage in the economic revolution equal in importance to the introduction of powered machines in the factories. It also went hand in hand with new advances in metallurgy—the Bessemer process in steel making (1856), the Siemens open hearth method (1864), and the Gilchrist Thomas process which, by the introduction of a limestone flux in 1879, made possible the use of phosphoric ores from south-east England and ended the dependence on coalfield iron ores. The demand for iron and steel for direct use for railmaking and locomotive building was enormous. Coal for steam power for the railways and for use in the multiplying numbers of blast furnaces was added to the demand from the factories and domestic users. The new 'iron horses' provided hitherto unheard-of fast, through transport to all parts of the country and, although the canals continued to fill a role in the slower movement of low-grade traffic, their decline was heralded as was that of the roads by 1850. As the second half of the nineteenth century got under way, the effects snowballed. Industry, finding national rather than local markets, flourished. Urban populations already swollen by the increase in mining and the movement of industry into the factories rose sharply from the 1840s and 1850s. The demand for food increased and agriculture in its turn was both stimulated and aided by better, fast transport. As time went on, it became zoned around the major towns so that milk and perishable foods could be produced as near as possible to their urban markets while beef cattle, sheep, and corn could be raised on more distant farms. Foreign foodstuffs and raw materials could also be brought in more easily and this, while it did much to maintain industry away from the ports, also in time brought depression into some branches of English farming. The railways provided a network which eventually reached almost every place in the land and provided fast, relatively cheap transport on a scale previously unknown.

The changes in the map of Cheshire which had begun with the revolution in industry in east Cheshire were now accelerated and added to. The Mersey rail tunnel between Liverpool and Birkenhead (1886) completed the series of river crossings of the Mersey which carried rail connections between Lancashire and Cheshire at Runcorn, Warrington, and Stockport, and across the Dee at Chester and Hawarden Bridge. Growth followed or was made possible near all these crossing points. Stockport with its great railway viaduct more than 100 feet high, underwent a marked expansion following the opening of the Crewe–Manchester line, and registered a population of 34,000 in 1851 as compared with 28,000 in 1841. It already had a head start compared with any other town in Cheshire, and the railway brought a further bonus.

When the railways reached Chester in the 1840s, the trade and industry of the city were far from flourishing. Silting had again become a serious problem and the linen trade, which was considerable in the eighteenth century, had so far declined by the mid-nineteenth that the Linenhall had been converted into a cheese mart, while in 1850 only one glover was left instead of the 200 hands employed in gloving in 1810. The effect of the railway was not immediate, but it ushered in a period when Chester's centrality was to be still further enhanced and one in which industry and trade, soon to be supplemented by tourism, were to be rescued from the depression which they suffered in the early part of the nineteenth century. Expansion outside the city walls had been slight up to 1800, but with the building of the General Station where formerly had flourished fields and gardens around Flookersbrook, there began a phase of rapid expansion in Flookersbrook itself and in Newtown and Hoole. Industries followed, but never on such a scale as to dominate the character of this ancient and beautiful city, and its population which was 16,000 in 1801 is now 59,000 (1961) making it the fourth town in order of size in the county.

A number of places in Cheshire received a fillip with the coming of the railways, and others including some of the older market towns less favourably situated, suffered a relative setback. The outstanding example of a town which was created purely as the result of the coming of the railways is Crewe where, prior to 1837, there were only a few scattered farms in the wide expanse of farming country

Railway line still in operation
Railway line now operating goods services only (1970)
Railway line now closed (1970)

11. THE RAILWAYS OF CHESHIRE

To Buxton

Stalybridge
1849
1846
1841
1857
STOCKPORT
1857
1845
MANCHESTER
Cheadle Hulme

Macclesfield
North Rode Jn.
1849
1849
To Leek and Uttoxeter
To Biddulph
To Stoke-on-Trent
Congleton
1848
Kidsgrove
To Stoke-on-Trent

Silverdale Colliery
To Birmingham and London

1842
1852

ALTRINCHAM
1853
1862
Knutsford
1863
NORTHWICH
1867
1837
Over and Wharton L.N.W.R.
Winsford and Over
1869
1870
CREWE
1848
1837
1858
1863
To Market Drayton
Nantwich

WARRINGTON
Weaver Jn.
1869
Helsby
1869
1850
1869
Tattenhall Jn.
1840
WIDNES
RUNCORN
To Liverpool

To Shrewsbury
WHITCHURCH
1872

Ellesmere Port
1863
1874
CHESTER
1846
To Wrexham

Hooton
1840
1866
1849
1848
To Mold

BIRKENHEAD
1840
1896
To Wrexham

New Brighton
1888
1896
Neston
To Holyhead
1878
West Kirby
1896
To Wrexham

0   10 Miles

60

between the two market towns of Nantwich and Sandbach. On 4 July 1837, the first train whistled triumphantly into a temporary station in the township of Crewe amid great rejoicing, but the real beginnings of the town were due to the building of the Grand Junction Works opened in the neighbouring township of Monks Coppenhall which, in 1877, was incorporated as the town of Crewe. Crewe station remained outside the borough boundary until 1936. From 148 inhabitants (in Monks Coppenhall township) in 1831, and 203 in 1841, its growth was rapid, reaching 4,500 in 1851, 42,000 in 1901, and 53,000 (making it the fifth town in Cheshire) in 1961.

XV

The Industrial Revolution in East Cheshire

Until the early eighteenth century, Cheshire like most of England was a largely rural county with a scattering of country towns, only Chester being of appreciable size. Industries of many types were widespread, but all were powered by water (or wind) or were operated by hand or, occasionally, by animals. It was the discovery of the way to use steam power which marked the watershed between the old order and the new. Steam was raised by coal. The Darbys at Coalbrookdale in Shropshire successfully used coke to smelt iron ore. Iron in the early days of powered industry came mainly from the ores in the Coal Measures. Hence, a new 'coalfield geography' began to dominate Britain, and an entirely new set of industrial towns sprang up, some based on old market towns, but others growing where there might previously have been no settlement at all.

In east Cheshire, the new industrial growth was based first on textiles. The making of woollen cloth has been practised from the Bronze Age. In the Middle Ages the industry became the most lucrative in England and, although Cheshire was not at all important in this, a number of places in and near the Pennines could boast very early woollen industries. A Stockport charter of 1220 mentions fullers, both Macclesfield and Congleton had fulling mills in the Middle Ages, and in the fifteenth century Congleton was making wool cloth and woollen gloves. They were cottage industries and so continued both in town and country into the eighteenth century, spinning by hand, weaving on hand-operated wooden looms, and fulling in water-powered mills. Silk buttons were made in Stockport and Macclesfield in the seventeenth century and there were hatters in Manchester and Stockport. Cotton had been imported from the sixteenth century, but most cotton piece goods were imported until new steam-powered spinning frames were introduced by Arkwright from 1769.

The mechanization of the silk industry began when John Lombe copied from the Italians a water-powered machine for throwing silk thread in Derby. On the expiry of the patent in 1732, Stockport became the first town in the country to set up a silk mill (leased for a thousand years!) using this machine, and in 1743, Charles Roe introduced it to Macclesfield in a mill which also included a dyehouse, a twisting house and a barn. Congleton followed suit in 1752 and, as in Macclesfield, it is said that James Brindley, the canal engineer, set up the machinery. By 1770, there were twelve silk mills in Stockport, but by 1800 most of them were converted to cotton. In Macclesfield and Congleton silk became the dominant industry with over 2,000 employees in Congleton in 1820, while in the same period Macclesfield's silk workers numbered over 10,000 (out of a total population of 21,000) and they worked a 62-hour week for which they were paid 11s. od. By that time, both towns were making a wide range of silk goods including ribbons, handkerchiefs, squares, and shawls. Piece-goods were soon to follow, and Congleton at the peak of the silk industry made ribbons, velvets, and satins.

In the 1760s, the improving wool crop of the Pennine moorlands encouraged the setting up of hatting shops and weaving sheds as well as swelling the cottage weaving industries at various places in the Cheshire Pennines—Marple, Bredbury, Hyde, Bollington, Handforth. At the same time, Hyde was using cotton with wool and Stockport and Congleton had both set up hemp

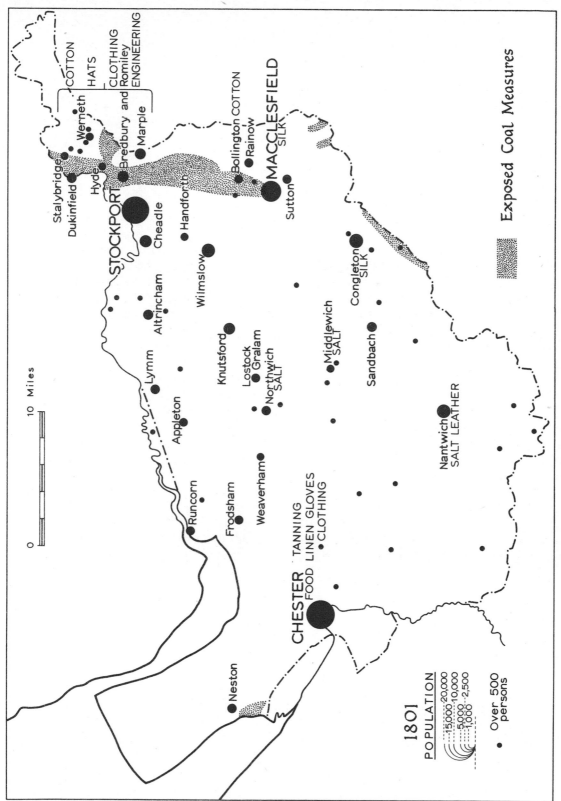

10 Miles

Exposed Coal Measures

COTTON
HATS
CLOTHING
Romiley
ENGINEERING

Stalybridge
Dukinfield
Hyde
STOCKPORT
Werneth
Bredbury and
Marple
Cheadle
Handforth
MACCLESFIELD
Bollington COTTON
Rainow
Sutton
SILK

Altrincham
Wilmslow
Lymm
Knutsford
Lostock
Gralam
Northwich
SALT
Congleton
SILK
Middlewich
SALT
Sandbach

Appleton
Weaverham
Frodsham
Runcorn
Nantwich
SALT LEATHER

Neston

CHESTER
FOOD
TANNING
LINEN GLOVES
CLOTHING

1801
POPULATION
15,000—20,000
10,000
5,000——2,500
1,000——2,500
Over 500 persons

12. POPULATION AND INDUSTRIES IN 1801

63

industries. The late eighteenth century saw many of the revolutionary developments in textile machinery—Crompton's Mule in 1779, and Cartwright's power loom (later improved) in 1785. In 1803–13, William Horrocks evolved the first all-metal power loom. Coal to raise steam and iron ore to provide the iron for the machines were available locally from the Lancashire-Cheshire coalfield and from North Staffordshire; and the textile industries, which had of necessity ceased to operate in cottages when heavy machinery was introduced, grew even more rapidly when steam power vastly increased the speed of output. In 1783, copper cylinder printing began to be used for patterning cottons, and in 1799 the bleaching process was reduced from months to days. Only, however, after 1830 were many factories adopting machine tools and abandoning their old methods and machines, and from that date progress was speeded up. By 1822, cotton was the staple industry of Stockport, and from 1800 Hyde and other cotton towns of north-east Cheshire sprang up around their mills, Hyde's population expanding from a mere 830 in 1800 to over 11,000 in 1830. Cotton was also introduced into Macclesfield and Congleton in the 1780s, but it declined in the slump following the Napoleonic Wars and was not revived in Macclesfield. In Congleton, silk and cotton continued side by side until silk was ousted

after 1930 by man-made fibres. Both towns are still dominated by the textile trade, whereas in Stockport, apart from hatting, textiles have declined in favour of engineering and allied trades.

Iron and steel, copper, and lesser manufactures such as leather also played a part in the early industrialization of east Cheshire towns. Copper ores from Alderley Edge were smelted in both Macclesfield and Congleton from 1758, and in Havannah and Bosley from about 1808. But these industries were comparatively short-lived and it was iron and steel and the industrial complex of related trades which were to become the second major cornerstone of industrial Stockport from the mid-nineteenth century. In Congleton, there were forges in 1750 and agricultural implements were made in 1773, and during the modern period numerous branches of engineering have multiplied in both towns, those of Stockport being far the larger. The major expansion of the iron and steel industries in this country dated from the middle of the nineteenth century, but the Gilchrist Thomas process made possible from the 1870s the use of ores from the newer strata of the Jurassic rocks in a belt from north-east Yorkshire across the Midlands. Although it ended dependence on the dwindling Coal Measures ores, older centres of production like Stockport continued to be important engineering towns.

XVI

Salt Wiches and Chemical Towns

'In King Edward's time there was a Wich (Nantwich) in Warmundestrou hundred in which there was a well for making salt, and between the King and Earl Edwin there were 8 salthouses.' So wrote the recorder in the Domesday Book about one of Cheshire's oldest and most valuable assets— salt. From a lead pan inscribed DEVE and found at Northwich, it seems very probable that the Romans worked salt there, and tradition has it that the British already knew of it. The Welsh traded in Cheshire for salt for centuries calling Nantwich *Hellath Wen*, the White Salt Town, and Northwich *Hellath Ddu*, the Black Salt Town. This most valuable of Cheshire's mineral products has certainly been used for hundreds of years. It formed the basis of one of her oldest industries, supplying domestic needs, and being used in the preparation of hides and skins, Before modern methods such as refrigeration were applied to the preservation of food, salt was invaluable in preserving meat for winter use after the autumn thinning of the herds. As modern industrial processes developed, it became one of the principal raw materials in the important alkali and soda manufactures which expanded in mid-Cheshire and the Mersey Basin in the nineteenth century.

Salt is extracted either as brine or rock salt. Brine may well up naturally from springs or boreholes (wild brine), but in recent times water injected into the rock salt bed has been pumped out again as brine. Rock salt was first discovered at Marbury near Northwich about 1670 and the first pit as far as is known was sunk by 1720; prior to this brine was the sole source. The early industry was carried on in the three 'Wiches'—Nantwich, Middlewich, and Northwich—all in the Northwich Basin of the Keuper Marls. These are beds laid down in hot desert conditions and the salt, which occurs at two successive depths, represents dried salt lakes from that period. In the 'bullaries' or salt houses of the premodern period, 'briners' led the brine into lead pans and it was then boiled with wood as a fuel. When the water had evaporated, 'wallers' raked out the salt deposit which remained. In the Middle Ages, the King and the Earl of Chester claimed a portion of the revenue, but it was still a sufficient source of wealth to ensure that anyone of note owned at least one salt house in one of the Wiches. According to Leland, there were 300 salt workers in 'Namptwyche' in the early sixteenth century and this must have been the peak period of Nantwich salt production. About 1530, there were 400 salt houses; in 1605, 216; and in 1624 only 108. William Smith, writing in 1580, said 'Nantwich is accounted the greatest town in Cheshire, next to Chester', and it was not until the late seventeenth or early eighteenth century that it was overtaken by Stockport. Camden in 1590 described it as 'the best built town in the county', and to this day its church and its half-timbered houses make it a place of outstanding charm and historic interest and beauty. In 1605, when Nantwich had 400 salt houses, Northwich had 113 and Middlewich 107, but gradual decline set in and the last Nantwich salt works was closed in 1856, though brine baths were used there medicinally until a few years ago. By contrast, Northwich was in the ascendant. Brine springs were discovered at Winsford in 1700, and in the late 1770s another part of the salt field yielded its first brine at Lawton and Wheelock. At nearby Sandbach, salt-making dates mainly from the 1870s. In the nineteenth and twentieth centuries, Sandbach brine was to become commercially significant, but in the eighteenth and early nineteenth centuries it was Northwich which led in output, with Middlewich as a minor producer. From 1700 onwards, numerous salt pits were sunk in the Marston–Witton district. The Great Marston Salt Mine was opened in 1780 when the lower bed of rock salt was first tapped. The salt industry was at last breaking out of medievalism. By 1638 or earlier, Nantwich substituted iron pans for lead, and coal began to replace wood as fuel. In 1682, Northwich produced over 12,000 bushels of salt a week, Middlewich 4,300, and Nantwich 4,200. Some went out on the old salt roads to nearby counties but an increasing amount went down the Weaver to join the growing stream of Mersey exports. A Frodsham refinery was opened before 1694, and one at Liverpool followed. Despite the tax imposed in that year, salt was recognized in Lancashire as well as in Cheshire as a profitable commodity. By the early eighteenth century English salt was shipped from the Mersey to Ireland, the Scandinavian countries, the Low countries and the Baltic, challenging French salt as its quality improved. The Cheshire field was the only extensive deposit of salt worked in Britain, most other domestic supplies being from evaporated sea-water. It was admirably situated in relation to coal supplies from Lancashire which at first were brought in by packhorse until the cost of coal transport became too heavy, and Lancashire refiners set up in effective competition by refining salt near to their coal. Water transport was good, but it was soon to be better, and with the canalization of the Weaver, open to traffic from 1732, and the growing importance of Liverpool's overseas trade, prospects were splendid. The construction of the St. Helens canal, the Mersey and Irwell navigation, and the Bridgewater Canal gave still better water transport in the Mersey–south Lancashire area. Similarly, the Trent and Mersey canal extended communications by water into Cheshire and the Trent valley, notably with

the north Staffordshire coalfield from which coal was carried to the refineries (and later to the chemical industry) and to which salt was brought on return journeys for use in glazing as the pottery industry grew. By 1817, the salt refiners were the principal buyers of St. Helens coal, and a triangular trade sprang up, Cheshire salt, St. Helens coal, and Liverpool refineries providing its points. The credit for the massive increases in the salt trade in the eighteenth century is attributed to Liverpool, total shipments from the Weaver rising from 58,000 tons in 1792–3 to 106,000 in 1799–1800. Total production of salt from the Cheshire field rose from 15,000 tons in 1732 to 150,000 in 1800, 500,000 in 1840, and and 1,000,000 in 1870. By the last date, Winsford, Sandbach, and Wheelock were making substantial contributions to the total, Winsford equalling Northwich. By the mid-nineteenth century, Middlewich had increased, Winsford reduced its output. That of Sandbach had also increased, and a brine pipeline had been constructed to carry the raw brine to Runcorn.

Much of the later story of salt is bound up with the development of the chemical industry, especially with the branches concerned with alkalis and soda. Sodium chloride or common salt is the basic material from which are derived caustic soda (used in soap manufacture), soda ash and crystals (washing soda), and sodium silicate or waterglass (used in soap making, in glues, size, paints and pottery manufacture). The early chemical industry based on salt used the Leblanc process by which alkalis were made from solid salt, using limestone, vitriol, and coal. In turn, alkali was manufactured from soda by Gossage's causticization process (before electrolysis was used). As early as the 1820s, soda ash and soda crystals were produced at St. Helens, Earlstown, Runcorn, and Widnes, and it was this last town which clung longest to Leblanc methods in the manufacture of alkalis and soda. As early as 1830, the Mersey Basin led British production of glass, and soap had become a valuable export, its production in the North second only to that of London.

The major development of the chemical industries, however, dates from the mid-nineteenth century. By that time, advances in the chemical sciences made possible the full development of the growing advantages of the Mersey Basin. The late eighteenth and early nineteenth centuries had enhanced the positions of the mid-Mersey towns by the construction of canals, coal production had increased on the south Lancashire field, the port of Liverpool had long outstripped Chester and was growing rapidly, its trade bringing in a constantly widening range of raw materials for industry. Population and manufacture were advancing in south Lancashire and north-east Cheshire and demanding more goods, and the railways were opening up a new era in transport.

Not only salt but coal was becoming important in the production of chemicals as research in coal-tar derivatives developed between 1838 and 1860, to produce oils, creosote, and especially dyes and colourants needed in the textile industry. The first chemical works were opened at Widnes in 1847, and Widnes continued as the main seat of the chemical industry until after World War I. In the 1830s, Runcorn was making a variety of things—ropes, slates, timber products and, among them, acids. In the 1850s and early 1860s, tanning and soap-making were the main branches of the chemical trade in which Runcorn was engaged, and already it was a growing manufacturing town. The extension of the Bridgewater Canal in 1767 and the link-up with the Trent and Mersey in 1791 increased the usefulness of the Weaver Navigation which had been opened to traffic sixty years previously. In 1803, the Old Quay Canal connected Runcorn and Warrington, and in 1807 the short Weston Canal made it possible for vessels to enter the Mersey at Weston Point where the Old Basin was constructed in 1830. The opening of the railway line from Crewe to Liverpool in 1869 gave the town good communications in all directions, and it was at about that date that soap manufacture in Runcorn declined in favour of heavy chemicals.

The new Solvay (or Ammonia-soda) process, using brine instead of salt with limestone, ammonia, and coke as the other materials, yielded a cheaper and purer soda ash, and there was no obnoxious sulphur containing solid waste. The process was evolved in Belgium between 1856 and 1866, and depended on the gas and coke industries. An energetic and far-seeing young man named Ludwig Mond obtained a licence to manufacture in Britain by this process in 1873, and in 1874 set up his works on the large Winnington Hall estate together with John Brunner. These joint founders of the firm of Brunner Mond, one of the forerunners of Imperial Chemical Industries, brought about the change in Northwich from a salt town to a chemical town, with fifty per cent of the present population dependent on the manufacture of chemicals. There were early difficulties, but the Northwich enterprise continued to grow and during the 1880s and 1890s the firm absorbed similar works which had been set up to the south and east at Middlewich, Sandbach, and Lostock Gralam.

In the 1890s, chlorine and caustic soda began to be produced by the electrolysis of brine. There was a simultaneous development of both mercury and diaphragm cells in England, on the Continent, and in U.S.A. Hargreaves and Bird began this type of production at Farnworth and, following the success of their pilot plant, formed the General Electrolytic Alkali Company with a works at Cledford Bridge near Middlewich, where production began in 1899. Leaders in the mercury cell field were Castner, an American, and Kellner (Austrian). With backing from the British Aluminium Company at Oldbury, they established a mercury cell plant at Weston Point near Runcorn in 1895, thus advancing the development of Runcorn as a chemical town. Weston Point had admirable water communications and land was cheap and plentiful, but land communications were even poorer than at Runcorn itself. Soft water, essential for the electrolysis of brine, was another problem, but this was solved by Liverpool making available water from the Lake Vyrnwy pipeline which crosses the Mersey between Runcorn and Warrington. Roads to Weston Point were only improved from 1919, and a branch railway reached it from Runcorn only in 1922; although the Transporter Bridge had given a Mersey crossing by road to Runcorn in 1905. Meanwhile, the Leblanc process, faced with growing opposition from the Solvay process, consolidated to form the United Alkali Company, which continued to produce by this method until 1914.

Long before the I.C.I. merger in 1926, Widnes, Runcorn, and Northwich had become established as heavy chemical towns, and Middlewich and Sandbach together with the village of Wheelock extended the chemical area south-eastward. Prior to the dominance of chemicals, metals, engineering, and leather had been important in the middle Mersey towns and these have continued, notably the last, which has also survived in Nantwich and Sandbach. But salt and chemicals remained the dominant theme in the economic life of the Cheshire saltfield and the lower Weaver in the nineteenth century. In each of the towns concerned, urban expansion resulted, in some dramatically. Runcorn which, according to King's *Vale Royal* had been nothing but a 'Fair parish

church, a parsonage, and a few scattered tenements' in 1656, blossomed into a small riverside resort in the early nineteenth century, only to be rudely shifted from this rural role as the noxious fumes of the chemical works drove away its more elegant visitors from the 1820s onwards. Its population doubled between 1801 (1,474) and 1821 (3,103), doubling again by 1861 (6,000). It reached its first peak in 1891 when it was over 20,000, but declined to 16,491 in 1901, when progress had slowed down and the effects of a narrowing range of industries was being felt.

In Northwich, the extensive subsidence which is an unhappy legacy from the period of uncontrolled salt and brine extraction, has prevented northward expansion, and large flashes, that is, small lakes forming in subsided ground, flank that side of the town. Population in Northwich township numbered less than 2,000 in both 1801 and 1851 but the town had already spread to adjoining townships and in 1851 the true urban population totalled 8,533. There was a sharp increase in the 1870s and 1880s after the establishment of the Brunner Mond Works but after that it slowed down and has only grown slowly since 1901 to a variable—and often declining —total of about 19,000. Nantwich, Middlewich, and Sandbach, remain small towns. Nantwich has only just passed 10,000, Sandbach 9,000, and Middlewich 6,000, while Winsford, prior to its recent expansion remained intermediate with 12,000.

XVII

Ships and Industry on Merseyside

The last industrial area of major importance to develop in Cheshire was Merseyside. In 1801, the entire hundred of Wirral had only 4,683 inhabitants. The largest place was Neston on Deeside (1,486) followed by Bebington (406), Tranmere (353), Eastham (348), and Ness (347). No other place had a population of 300 and only six more exceeded 200. It was villages, hamlets, and green fields all the way. Yet by 1851, Wirral's population totalled 50,000 and in 1961 over 407,000. Of this last total, the four Merseyside boroughs accounted for 341,000, twenty-five per cent of the total for the county as compared with twenty-three per cent (323,000) in the conurbation of north-east Cheshire. And the spread of settlement is still active.

The story of Cheshire's Merseyside growth is, of course, closely linked with that of the Lancashire shore. Liverpool grew rapidly in the late eighteenth century, its population rising from 34,000 in 1773 to 54,000 in 1790. Its trade and shipping were active and prosperous, yet the opposite shore of the estuary was like a far country. Here the tides race dangerously through the narrow opening, and, although in 1330 an ancient right of ferry had been confirmed by royal charter to the Prior of Birkenhead to carry passengers and goods for ever 'across the said arm of the sea', and although it thus became a part of the King's highway which must be maintained, few cared to cross these uncertain waters. The Cheshire shore of the estuary is remarkably straight, but two creeks, Wallasey Pool the longer and Tranmere Pool the lesser, break into its even line opposite the pool from which Liverpool took the latter part of its name. Between the two inlets on the Cheshire side is a small peninsula on which are the ruins of Birkenhead Priory. There was not even a sizeable hamlet there and in 1801 the tiny township supported only 110 souls.

Change began quite dramatically within a decade. In 1817, the first steam ferryboat began service between Tranmere and Liverpool, and in 1822 a second was plying across the Mersey from Woodside. The journey took ten minutes, and soon the stream of immigrants from the Lancashire side began to settle near the ferry termini. In 1821 at Birkenhead there were 200 counted at the census, but still the movement was only a trickle when a youth called William Laird who had gone to live in Liverpool in 1810, bought up land near Wallasey Pool. The year was 1824 and in that same year he built an iron works there. Laird was a true man of vision. He it was who saw the possibilities of Birkenhead becoming a great port like Liverpool. The position was similar except that it was not backed by a hinterland where textiles were already important but, as later developments proved, two other great industries were to justify Laird's faith in the future of Cheshire's Merseyside—shipbuilding and chemicals.

In 1828, he got his first shipbuilding order, and the building of iron vessels which began the following year was a further factor in his success. Within a decade, and at this vital period in ship design, the yard had completed seventeen ships. He proved to be a gifted ship designer and before his death in 1873, the firm had turned out many good ships for coastal and cross-channel trade. But he also had vision as regards the growth of the town which was to rise around and behind Wallasey Pool, and instead of the haphazard and ugly building which so often accompanied industrial expansion, he envisaged a town with dignity and regularity of plan and engaged Graham, an Edinburgh architect, who designed Hamilton Square and the surrounding streets, houses, and industrial sectors. The rate of growth was phenomenal —2,569 in 1831, 8,223 in 1841, and over 24,000 by mid-century.

From the beginning, Laird saw the need for specialization in the ship yards, and some considerable part of his success was due to the army of smiths, platers, riveters, caulkers, and shipwrights who were trained in the yards. Another urgent need was good communications. George Stephenson first surveyed the Birkenhead–Chester railway route in 1830 but it was only opened to traffic in 1840. In 1844, dock building began, and in 1857 Birkenhead came jointly with Liverpool under the management of the Mersey Docks and Harbour Board. In that year, Laird's moved from the site near the present Victoria Dock which had become too restricted, to the present site of the Cammell Laird shipyard where deep water three-quarters of a mile wide gives ample launching room. Dock lines were built to speed up traffic in 1859, and Cheshire Lines reached Birkenhead docks in 1870. The development of good communications, apart from these early routes, was by no means rapid, but a number of local railways date from the 1880s to the turn of the century, including the underground line to Liverpool (1886). Only in 1926–34 was the first road tunnel built.

Other shipyards, many supporting industries and port activities followed as the century advanced. Metal industries and many branches of engineering, especially marine engineering, paints and lubricants, furniture, pulleys and cranes were linked with the shipyard. As shipping lines began to operate from the port as they did from the 1850s and 1860s, imports grew and typical port industries based on imported raw materials such as timber, tropical foodstuffs, grain, cattle, vegetable oils and mineral products sprang up. Sawmills, food processing such as flour

milling and the making of animal products resulted but, among the multiplicity of new activities, one of the early ones and one which was to be in some sense a pointer to future developments on Cheshire's Merseyside, was the establishment of a soap factory by W. H. Lever in 1888. Another man of vision, he built the garden village of Port Sunlight to house his work people, a historic example of advanced architectural and social planning. This extension of the chemical industry downriver, was another of the early indicators of the lines Merseyside industry was to follow. Later also, Lever Brothers were to buy out Gossage's soap works in Widnes and move that industry to Warrington, so concentrating the soap factories of the Mersey Basin into two main centres.

The latter part of the nineteenth century saw not only the expansion of Birkenhead, but the outward spread of population from that first urban centre. Birkenhead itself spread along the coast and inland absorbing neighbouring townships. Increasing ferry facilities encouraged a south-eastward move along Merseyside, first into Bebington where the Port Sunlight works were built, and which mustered nearly 3,000 inhabitants by 1851. A larger movement was along the open coast into Seacombe, Liscard, and New Brighton which by 1850 was 'a modern bathing place' in Wallasey township. Between them they brought up the population of Wallasey parish to over 8,000 at that date, and Wallasey became the second County Borough of Wirral in 1913. It extends north of the Great Float which separates it from Birkenhead, and an industrial belt is located in that part of the town, but the resort and residential aspects remain.

Perhaps to Merseyside rather than to any other major Cheshire area have come large numbers of migrants from other parts of the British Isles. A growth rate which by 1861 had been sufficient to sketch out the main lines of Wirral's more northerly urban settlements could only be accounted for by vast numbers of newcomers. Census data are lacking for the early years on sources of immigration, but later figures and an analysis of surnames make it clear that Irish predominated. In addition, people came in from Lancashire and other parts of Cheshire, from North Wales and, in lesser numbers, from Scotland. In the last hundred years, the urban and suburban settlement area has extended still further up-estuary through Bromborough towards Eastham and along the north coast to Hoylake and West Kirby, leaving the Dee shore far behind in terms of population, although more recently suburbs have spread, very modestly, towards Heswall. Neston, until 1820 the only town in Wirral, remained a quiet country town, left far behind by the massive settlement of Merseyside.

The second story of urban growth in Wirral—that of Ellesmere Port, belongs largely to the twentieth century, but it began and was based on two earlier events. The opening of the Ellesmere Canal (now part of the Shropshire Union) from Chester to the Mersey in the 1790s and the naming of its outlet after Ellesmere in Shropshire have already been mentioned. In 1894, the opening of the Manchester Ship Canal which terminated at Eastham three miles down river, was the second factor which was to bring the population of Ellesmere Port and Whitby from the figure of 1,261 recorded in 1901 to 32,000 in 1951, and to convert this once lonely stretch of coast into a major oil terminal and industrial centre. It links the development of the mid-Mersey Basin with that of the lower estuary.

XVIII

Chester

If there is one place more than another that embodies Cheshire's history, that place is most surely Chester. City and county town, two thousand years have gone by since it came to birth, for it is now certain that the British or Celtic people once occupied this site and all the country round it. This was confirmed as recently as 1966 when excavations conducted by Mr. D. F. Petch discovered plough marks under the Roman parade ground. The name Deva itself has Celtic origins, and when the Roman legions became established there, the British name Caerlleon—City of the Legions—was given to it by the British Cornovii who inhabited Cheshire at that time.

The reasons why the Romans chose this site—at the head of the Dee estuary, at its lowest bridging point, and at a place ideally suited to the planned advance into the Welsh Hills and along the vital North Welsh coastal route—were the ones which caused the Normans and Edwardians in the Middle Ages to make it the administrative centre of the new and powerful earldom, and the spearhead of their advance into North Wales. Time has altered some of these advantages, re-emphasizing some, such as its centrality, weakening others by the silting of the estuary and by the work of modern engineers who have been able to bridge the Dee below the city at Queensferry. But, apart from its military role and the decline of the port, Chester has increased and widened its central functions since the Middle Ages, and although it is shorn of large portions of the early Norman county, it retains its place as a regional capital and has added many new roles and activities during the last four to five hundred years.

Chester is unique in Britain as a present-day city which has kept the major features of a Roman legionary fortress plan as the basis of its own layout. The York of today has no relationship whatever to the buried fortress below its narrow, winding streets, and Caerleon in Monmouthshire, the third of the great legionary fortresses is only a large village built without regard to the underlying Roman lines. But in Chester, the north and east walls follow the exact line of the Roman walls for the builders of the Middle Ages used the foundations and the partially ruined Roman walls and built up from them. In addition, they lengthened them westward and southward, still keeping the 'playing card' plan, but pushing out the south-western angle to include the castle, so that the regular oblong form was slightly altered. Eastgate Street and Watergate Street lie along the main west-east road of the Roman fortress, and Northgate Street and Bridge Street follow the north-south line even to the break in the intersection at St. Peter's Church—'the High Cross'. This church was built on the site of the Roman Headquarters building, and near to St. Peter's was the Pentice, the administrative centre in the Middle Ages, and not far away, the nineteenth-century Town Hall was built.

The best way to see Chester and to absorb the atmosphere of this historic city, is to walk the full circuit of the walls and to trace from them some of the main features of its layout. The Roman wall is still followed from St. Martin's Gate (where the new Inner Ring Road crosses it in the north) to the New Gate in the east beyond which is the Roman amphitheatre. From St. Martin's Gate, the medieval ramparts were built to include a strip of approximately 200 yards wide west of the old Roman wall which has been traced by

22. Runcorn: the railway bridge and the new high-level bridge linking it with Widnes across the Mersey.

23. Crewe: the railway station and the junction of main lines.

24. Stanlow, Ellesmere Port: the new skyline of the petro-chemical industry – the Shell (South) Refinery.

excavation. The west wall, which runs from the Water Tower by the Water Gate to the Castle, was so aligned that the northern part lay near the harbour, though today the river is almost a quarter of a mile away. Nevertheless, this is still the part where the visitor can find evidence of the port activities. Near to it in the eighteenth century, Paradise Row and Crane Street were built to house the mariners, shipbuilders, anchormakers, and sailmakers. The port is now served by the New Cut of 1735–7, and the Mayor still has the additional title of Admiral of the Dee.

The medieval castle was replaced largely in the years 1789–1813 by the present structure. From the walls between it and the Watergate, the view is across the Roodee, now the Racecourse, but until about 1400 it was the head of the estuary and part of the port of Roman Deva and later of medieval Chester. The Castle was so placed as to command both the harbour and the only bridge which spanned the river in the pre-modern era. It now serves both as the Headquarters of the Cheshire Regiment and as the offices of some of the County Council departments, the rest being housed in the large new County Hall which is near to the south-western part of the city wall and was opened in 1957. The Old Dee Bridge built in the late thirteenth century replaced the one mentioned in the Domesday Book, and there may have been a Roman bridge on or near the site. Extensively repaired in the fourteenth century, it must have re-echoed to the martial tramp of thousands of feet, as time and again armies marched across it into Wales. The famous Mills of Dee were at its northern end and both bridge and mills were repaired many times, the mills finally being destroyed by fire in 1895.

From the Old Dee Bridge, the lower end of Bridge Street climbs steeply up to the Cross, and on the south side leads into Handbridge, one of the oldest parts of the city outside the walls. Here the river flows immediately below the line of the southern wall which is entirely medieval, and the wall soon turns north,

towards the East Gate, from which there is perhaps the finest view in Chester along the straight line of Eastgate Street and Watergate Street. A little further on, one has the best view of the Cathedral Church of St. Werburgh, a Benedictine abbey until the Dissolution, and on the north-eastern corner is the Phoenix Tower, now known as King Charles' Tower because Charles I is said to have watched from there the late stages of the battle of Rowton Moor in 1645. To the East lie the now extensive suburbs, the General Station and railway yards, industrial premises which sprang up in the nineteenth century in Flookersbrook, Newtown, and Hoole, and below the north wall in a deep, rock-cut channel are the waters of the old Chester Canal built in the 1770s and now part of the Shropshire Union Canal. The circuit of the walls is completed beyond the North Gate which, like the other city gates, has replaced the original medieval one.

Within the walls, the four major streets reveal more of the city's history. Half-timbered houses and inns are numerous, bearing testimony to the importance of the rebuilding which went on in the sixteenth and seventeenth centuries. Many houses have medieval, and some Roman, cellars and old interiors are numerous. One of the finest houses is Stanley Palace built in 1591 and so called because later it became the town house of the Stanleys of Alderley. It stands at the junction of Nicholas Street and Watergate Street and further to the east in Watergate Street are God's Providence House and Bishop Lloyd's House, the latter an exceptionally beautiful example of a frame building with elaborate carving. Inns were always important in this city where markets and commerce flourished, and became even more so in the coaching age; there are many fine old hostelries to bear witness to this, such as the Falcon and the Old King's Head in Lower Bridge Street.

The religious houses, other than St. Werburgh's, are mainly remembered in street names such as White Friars and Black

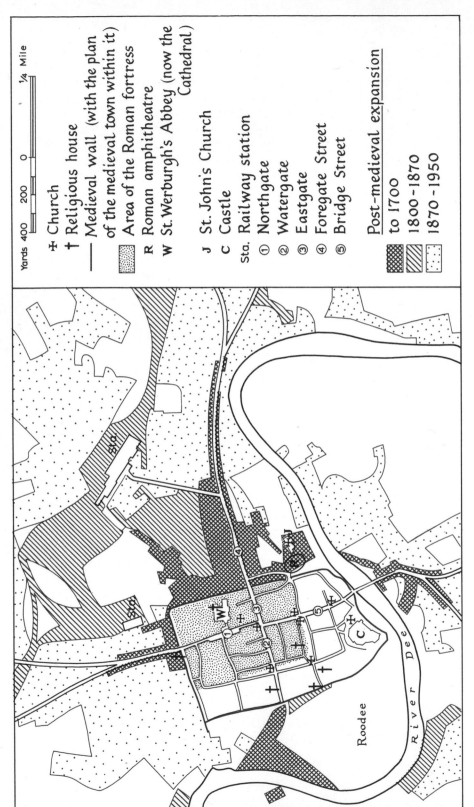

Yards 400 200 0   ¼ Mile

☩ Church
† Religious house
— Medieval wall (with the plan of the medieval town within it)
▦ Area of the Roman fortress
R Roman amphitheatre
W St. Werburgh's Abbey (now the Cathedral)
J St. John's Church
C Castle
sta. Railway station
① Northgate
② Watergate
③ Eastgate
④ Foregate Street
⑤ Bridge Street

Post-medieval expansion
     to 1700
     1800–1870
     1870–1950

Roodee

River Dee

13. CHESTER

74

Friars, but the old parish churches remain, and the most unusual of these is St. John's outside the city walls near the New Gate, not only on account of its architectural interest but because it was the cathedral church of Mercia in 1075–95 before the see was removed to Lichfield. The present cathedral is the richest storehouse of ecclesiastical architecture in the city.

The end of the Chester story is never reached for discovery follows on discovery, but one puzzle has defeated all attempts to solve it, that is, the origin of the Rows. These unique, quaint, and often beautiful raised pedestrian ways lining much of the main central thoroughfares are even more valuable today than formerly because they afford safe, covered ways for pedestrians and shoppers. They may date from the rebuilding after the fire of 1278, or have been built at different periods. They are for the most part now lined with shops, and offices, some of which were formerly private residences. During the latter part of the Middle Ages various trades tended to be grouped in one or other of the Rows and to take their names from them, for example, Fleshmongers' Row in Watergate Street and Mercers' Row in Bridge Street.

In addition to the main streets which divide the walled town into four quarters, there are many lesser roads and lanes. Of these, St. Werburgh's Street offers a fine view of the cathedral rising beyond the old houses which are a feature of the east side of this street. A considerable part of the plan of the medieval city has been altered, filling in the open spaces and gardens which occupied much of its area, and in many cases wiping out all traces of the older, narrow lanes. The eighteenth century saw considerable rebuilding, and many good Georgian houses can be seen as in Abbey Street, Abbey Square and Abbey Green. Two major roadways were cut in the nineteenth century diagonally across the grid plan which, until then, had been followed by every city street. One of the new diagonals was followed by Grosvenor Street and Grosvenor Road leading from the junction of Pepper Street and Bridge Street to Grosvenor Bridge which was built in 1832. The other was City Road which was made to give direct access to the General Station from Foregate Street. The former became the main route out of Chester to North Wales and led to the growth of the Curzon Park suburb near the gates of Eaton Hall. Beyond the walls, there is little now to differentiate the later growth of commercial and residential districts from those of many other nineteenth- and twentieth-century urban extensions, but within the heart of the city none could mistake the historic importance of Chester. As a county town, once the administrative centre of a palatine earldom and of a palatinate county which kept its palatinate courts until 1830, as a once great port, as a market and trading centre, as an assay town until 1686, as a route centre and the gateway to North Wales, as a cathedral city from the sixteenth century, as the Headquarters of Western Command, and as a town with County Courts and the Courts of Assize, Chester has grown with each successive century. In the 1506 Charter, the city was constituted a county of itself and, as such, has a Sheriff, Recorder, and Court of Sessions. It has beauty and dignity from ages past and it is part of the heritage not only of Cheshire but of Britain.

XIX

Cheshire in the Twentieth Century

History is forever in the making, and the twentieth century has been, if anything, even more eventful than those which came before. As the pace of discovery and invention speed up, new vistas open, and in no spheres has this been more evident than in industry, communications, and transport, and Cheshire has been vitally affected by the continuing technical revolution of the present century.

Changes are too numerous to mention in full, but there are some 'watersheds' more important than others which divide the old from the new. The revolution towards modern transport which brought traffic back to the roads was heralded by the invention of the internal combustion engine which was first used on a tricycle in 1885, and from that date, though at first slowly, was applied to motor vehicles. It was, however, the Railway Strike of 1911 which first demonstrated the fact that industry and commerce in this country might once more be served by road transport. After World War I both road and air transport advanced. The war period was indeed a 'watershed' in human history.

In 1926, the Electricity Supply Act was passed, and from that date, the numerous small concerns and supply lines which had until then supplied relatively restricted parts of the country with electricity were eventually linked up into a nationwide grid. From the early 1930s, industry gradually began to adapt itself both in method and place, for with electric power available anywhere, the 'coalfield geography' of the nineteenth century began to break down. Counties which, like Cheshire, had little or no coal, could expand industrially as never before.

The electro-technical age brought a vast train of results. Radio, television, electrical engineering, and advancing methods in the chemical industry were among them. In addition, new materials, notably rayon, followed by other and still more revolutionary man-made fibres, plastics, chemicals, drugs, alloys, and so on, were introduced. Just as electricity, made available through the grid, freed power resources, so rapid developments in communications and transport freed raw materials, making them more quickly and more widely available.

In the history of communications another major 'watershed' was passed with the opening to traffic of the Manchester Ship Canal on the 1st January, 1894. Its value to Lancashire was soon made clear. More unexpected was the extent to which Cheshire would benefit from this great ocean canal. From a point two miles east of Runcorn bridge it is cut close to the Cheshire shore of the estuary as far as its terminus at Eastham Locks, and large ocean-going vessels can navigate its entire length. The county's second major inland waterway, the Weaver Navigation, has undergone continuous improvement during this century, and since 1935, it can take 500-ton coastal vessels and 450-ton barges up to Winsford as compared with 200-ton coastal vessels and 250-ton barges before the deepening of the channel. In addition, the electrification of the unique Anderton Lift in 1905, made traffic between the Weaver and the Trent and Mersey Canal quicker, easier, and more profitable. The Rusholme Report on canals and inland waterways (1954) put the Weaver Navigation in Group I, the group which had substantial traffic and which should be improved, and the Trent and Mersey in Group II, to be retained and improvement aimed at.

Railways have been increasingly challenged by road traffic since the 1930s, and the amalgamation into four main groups in 1923 did little to improve matters. In 1953, five years after nationalization as British Rail, the Transport Act called for modernization and this was begun two years later. Since then, electrification and liner freight traffic have been among the improvements made on certain main lines and in Cheshire, both the Crewe–Manchester and the Crewe–Liverpool routes were electrified by 1961. Unfortunately, there has also been extensive closure of routes, and although Cheshire has suffered less than many counties in this respect, line closures, restriction of certain lines to goods traffic only, and the closure of intermediate stations have brought hardship to rural areas and to the economic prospects of many small places.

On the other hand, road conditions such as surface, width, and straightness, have been given high priority. By-passes have been constructed at Chester, Cheadle, Northwich, and Congleton, and between Helsby and Shotwick a nine-mile stretch of entirely new road (A5117T) was opened as early as 1936. This links south-east Lancashire and north Cheshire with Wirral and North Wales without entering Chester, and is of particular value to the Merseyside towns and to North Wales. Its value, and that of other Cheshire roads, was further enhanced by the building of the high level bridge which replaced the old transporter at Runcorn from 1961—and thus made Runcorn a far more effective 'lowest bridging point' across the Mersey— and the opening in the following year of the Queensferry bridge across the Dee. The road tunnel between Liverpool and Birkenhead which was opened to traffic in 1934, carries a heavier load than any of the main bridging points, but both this and the Queensferry bridge are used by so many vehicles that duplication of the two was planned in the 1960s. In the east of Cheshire, the M6 motorway was completed and open to traffic in 1963 as part of the Birmingham–Preston route. By the end of the following year it had

already increased trade in the towns near to it and continues to do so. It enters the county near Barthomley, passing by Sandbach, Holmes Chapel, and Knutsford to Lymm. An east-west motorway is being built across north Cheshire.

Most of the changes which have taken place so far this century in sources of power, availability of raw materials, and transport have been favourable to the developing economy of Cheshire and—wars and depression periods apart—the general trend has been towards greater prosperity. Industries have multiplied and population has increased. The main natural resources of Cheshire are salt and agricultural produce, but it is now a long cry from the days when salt evaporation, cheese making, and tanning were its principal manufactures though food industries continue and are widespread. Salt, both as salt and as the basis of the spiralling chlorine and alkali branches of the chemical industry, remains of prime importance. The Weaver valley towns from Runcorn to Winsford, and the extension of the actively exploited salt field in the Middlewich–Sandbach area are together part of the most important chemical region of Britain. The other part, the Mersey Basin, now specializes also in oleo- and petro-chemicals in a belt extending from Birkenhead through Bromborough, Port Sunlight, and Ellesmere Port to Runcorn where the two lines hinge. This branch of the Mersey industry depends to a great extent on imported vegetable oils and petroleum. Each of these towns has its own water frontage and docks on the Mersey or the Ship Canal or both, and first class facilities exist for the importing of oils of both groups. Runcorn and Weston Point docks have been extended and in 1960, the new oil terminal was opened at Tranmere with a pipeline to Stanlow, a site on which there has been continuous expansion of the oil refining and processing plant by Shell since the 1920s. Development has also continued in the salt belt, still concentrating its main chemical production in the early years

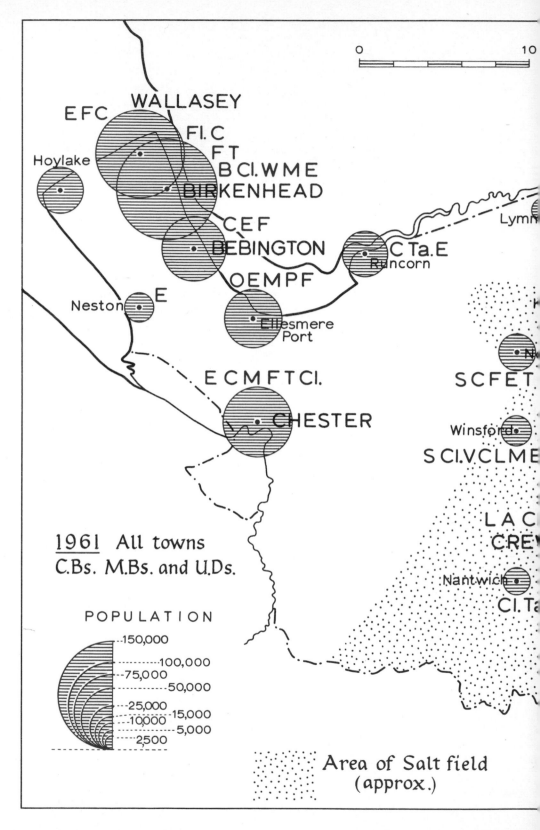

O ————————— 10

WALLASEY

E F C

Fl. C
FT
B Cl. W M E
BIRKENHEAD

Hoylake

C E F
BEBINGTON

C Ta. E
Runcorn

Lymn

Neston E

O E M P F
Ellesmere
Port

E C M F T Cl.

CHESTER

SCFET

Winsford

S Cl. V Cl. M E

L A C
CREW

Nantwick

Cl. Ta

<u>1961</u> All towns
C.Bs. M.Bs. and U.Ds.

POPULATION

150,000
100,000
75,000
50,000
25,000
15,000
10,000
5,000
2,500

Area of Salt field
(approx.)

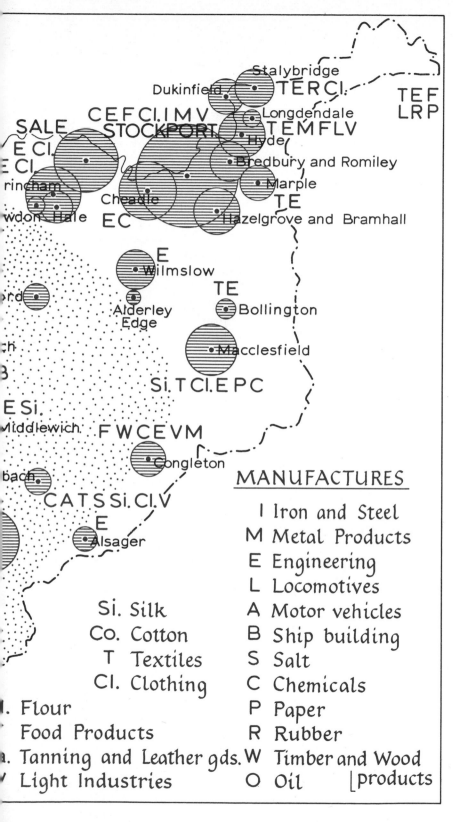

Stalybridge

Dukinfield TERCI.

TEF
LRP

CEFCI.IMV
SALE STOCKPORT

Longdendale
TEMFLV

E CI
E CI

Hyde

rincham

Bredbury and Romiley

Cheadle

Marple

wdon Hale EC

TE

Hazelgrove and Bramhall

E

Wilmslow

TE

ord

Bollington

Alderley
Edge

Macclesfield

ch

B

Si. T CI. E P C

E Si.

Middlewich

F W C E V M

Congleton

bach

MANUFACTURES

C A T S Si. CI. V

E

Alsager

I	Iron and Steel
M	Metal Products
E	Engineering
L	Locomotives
Si. Silk	A	Motor vehicles
Co. Cotton	B	Ship building
T Textiles	S	Salt
CI. Clothing	C	Chemicals

Si. Silk   A Motor vehicles
Co. Cotton   B Ship building
T Textiles   S Salt
CI. Clothing   C Chemicals
. Flour   P Paper
Food Products   R Rubber
. Tanning and Leather gds. W Timber and Wood
Light Industries O Oil   ⌊products

of the century at Runcorn and Northwich, both of which became dominated by chemicals.

The development of the techniques of brine electrolysis was one factor, and the industrial combines culminating in 1926 in the I.C.I. merger was the second factor which led to the extension and modernization of the chemical industries of these two towns. More recently, large scale plant has been set up by other firms between Middlewich and Sandbach, further extending the electro-chemical production of chlorine and alkali products.

The old textile belt of east Cheshire, concentrated in the Stockport area with its close-packed neighbouring towns, continues its now stabilized industry with modernization, and this applies also to Macclesfield, still dominated by textiles. More varied textile production continues in a broken arc through Congleton to Sandbach, Crewe, and Nantwich, with recent extension on Winsford's industrial estate. A number of other places in the county are linked with some branch or other of textiles and clothing, but the main area is still this eastern belt. The electrification of the Manchester–Crewe railway line and the opening of the M6 motorway have considerably improved communications in east Cheshire and have notably stimulated industrial development including light industries at Sandbach and Congleton.

Metal and engineering industries, like food and textiles, are widespread, but major centres stand out. Marine engineering dominates Birkenhead, and ship repairing at Runcorn, and specialized types of ship building at Northwich may be mentioned too. Road vehicles are now old-established at Sandbach; Rolls Royce cars came to Crewe in 1938, and the Vauxhall plant at Hooton Park (Ellesmere Port) sent out its first cars in 1966. Stockport is a major centre of general and textile engineering, and chemical engineering is carried on in the chemical towns, while Crewe remains a centre of railway engineering. Computers are made at Wins-

ford and there are nuclear reactors at Knutsford.

The last group that need be singled out, the light industries, are of every type that may be fitted into small plant. Their merits are that they are diverse and therefore act as a bolster to the economy of old towns formerly dependent on too narrow a range of products, that many in this category rank as consumer industries, and that they can be established quickly and usually successfully on the industrial estates which many councils are now setting up. They generally serve as adjuncts to a heavier industrial structure in the older towns as at Stockport, Crewe, and Northwich, and are found in the 'New Towns' of Runcorn and Congleton—one of which is a nineteenth-century town designated as such for expansion, and the other a medieval one. (Congleton was designated in 1947, Runcorn in 1964.)

No two towns have an identical history, but some of the principal types have already been suggested—the small country towns; the medieval centres and the nineteenth-century towns which have adopted an industrial economy; those with ports; and the county town, Chester. A glance at the population table following this section will show that some are now showing little change in total, some are declining slightly, and a number are entering on a growth period. Among these last may be mentioned another type which is a product of the late nineteenth or twentieth century or both: the town which is largely residential. Wilmslow, Cheadle, and Sale are examples in north-east Cheshire, Wallasey in Wirral, with Neston now following suit. But the most impressive example of a town which has arisen this century from the marshes, as did Birkenhead last century, is Ellesmere Port.

Ellesmere Port is Cheshire's outstanding success as the new town of this century. Known first as Netherpool, then as Whitby Locks after the cutting of the Ellesmere Canal in 1795, the name Ellesmere Port was first heard in about 1820. Railways reached it only in 1863, and it carried on a very small trade until the cutting of the Manchester Ship Canal. As the first place above Eastham where bulk cargo could be handled, its now excellent water communications began the period of real growth. It boasted only 1,261 residents in 1901, or 4,082 in the ecclesiastical parish, but in 1902 it was created an Urban District. By 1931, it had nearly 19,000 people and by the middle of 1969, this population had almost trebled, helped by overspill from Liverpool. An eventual total of 85,000 is expected. This remarkable build-up is based on a modernized port with a minimum depth of 30 feet of water at all times, road and rail on the quayside, and extensive warehousing and cranage. Behind it all, is a now gigantic group of mineral oil industries, the largest of which has developed a further set of port facilities at Stanlow. Petro-chemicals are the mainstay of Ellesmere Port and it is the largest oil-refining and paper-making centre in northern England. Vauxhall Motors are now a major concern there employing over 11,000 and in addition there are engineering firms, varied chemical products, and a number of light industries. The new Helsby-Shotwick road runs along its southern boundary and has revolutionized road communication which was formerly a weak point. It is not surprising that it became a Municipal Borough in 1955.

These three lines of towns—the eastern, the central, and the northern, together with Chester, constitute the town map of Cheshire. But there still remain, thankfully, unspoilt market centres such as Knutsford, Nantwich, Lymm, and Neston, and vast, if shrinking, acres of farmland, and a great heritage of rural beauty. Cheshire's long history is enshrined in her fields, her villages, and in her towns, old and new.

POPULATION OF CHESHIRE (in thousands)

	1801	1951	1961	mid-1966	mid-1969
County	191	1,258	1,368	1,473	1,512
County Borough					
Birkenhead	0·1	142	141	142	141
Chester	15	57	59	60	60
Stockport	14	141	142	141	140
Wallasey	0·2	101	103	103	101
Municipal Borough					
Altrincham	1	39	41	41	41
Bebington	0·4	47	52	55	57
Congleton	3	15	16	18	19
Crewe	0·1[1]	52	53	52	51
Dukinfield	1	18	17	17	17
Ellesmere Port	0·1	32	44	51	56
Hyde	1	31	31	38	38
Macclesfield	8	35	37	40	41
Sale	0·8	43	51	55	55
Stalybridge	1	22	21	21	21
Urban District					
Alderley Edge	0·4	3	3	4	4
Alsager	0·2	5	7	9	10
Bollington	1	5	5	5	6
Bowdon	0·3	3	4	4	4
Bredbury and Romiley	2	17	21	27	28
Cheadle and Gatley	2	31	45	53	57
Hale	0·7	12	14	16	16
Hazel Grove & Bramhall	1	19	30	34	35
Hoylake	0·1[2]	30	32	32	32
Knutsford	2	6	9	10	11
Longdendale	0·9	4	4	7	10
Lymm	1	6	7	8	9
Marple	2	13	16	22	24
Middlewich	1	6	6	7	8
Nantwich	3	8	10	11	11
Neston	1	9	11	15	16
Northwich	1	19	19	19	18
Runcorn	1	23	26	30	31
Sandbach	1	9	9	10	12
Wilmslow	3	19	21	27	28
Winsford	0·8[3]	12	12	17	22
Wirral	–	17	21	25	26
Rural District					
Bucklow		11	17	21	21
Chester		25	28	33	33
Congleton		13	14	16	18
Disley		2	2	3	3
Macclesfield		19	23	26	26
Nantwich		27	27	30	34
Northwich		35	39	40	42
Runcorn		35	39	40	42
Tarvin		14	14	16	17
Tintwistle		1	1	1	1

N.B. The figures are not in every case for comparable areas, especially those for 1801.

[1] Monks Coppenhall   [2] Little Meols   [3] Over

XX

A Short Dictionary of Cheshire Biography

BACK, Sir George (1796–1878), was born at Holly Vale, Stockport, and educated at Stockport Grammar School. He became a courageous and distinguished explorer, mainly in Arctic and sub-Arctic regions. From 1818–23, he accompanied Sir John Franklin on the first modern voyage round Spitzbergen, to the Coppermine river, and on a survey of the American Coast. He was later on the expedition which went in search of Ross. He was awarded the Gold Medal of the Royal Geographical Society and was knighted in 1838.

BEATTY, David, Viscount Borodale of Wexford, Baron Beatty of the North Sea and of Brooksby (1871–1936), was born at Howbeck Lodge, Stapeley, near Nantwich. He became Admiral of the Fleet, and during World War I was the hero of the battles of the Dogger Bank and of Jutland. He was made a Freeman of the City of Chester, and for his services in the Navy (he was then Sir David Beatty) an earldom was conferred on him.

BOOTH, Sir George, later first Baron Delamere of Dunham Massey (1622–84), succeeded the older Sir George who was created a baronet in 1611. As a Cromwellian he served in all the Protectorate parliaments, and supported the Parliamentary side in the Cheshire campaigns, but later became a Royalist and led the Cheshire rising of 1659. He was taken prisoner and confined in the Tower of London. After his release he was instrumental with others in bringing back Charles II to England and was made Baron in 1661 for his part in the Restoration.

BRADSHAW, John (1602–59), was born at Wibbersley Hall in the Goyt valley. He was educated at Bunbury and Middleton, and served as a clerk to an attorney in Congleton, eventually becoming Chief Justice of Chester, one of the judges for Wales, and a judge of the Sheriff's Court in London. He was president of the court which condemned Charles I to death and, when he died of the plague was given a magnificent funeral and buried in Westminster Abbey. But after the Restoration, his body was exhumed, hanged at Tyburn, and ingloriously buried there.

BRERETON, Sir William (1604–61), of Handforth Hall, was the Parliamentarian Commander in Cheshire during the Civil Wars. He was educated at Brasenose College, Oxford, and elected M.P. in 1628. He died at Croydon and was to have been buried at Cheadle, but it is said that his body was carried away in a flood at a river crossing on the journey from London.

BROWNSWERD, John (1540?–89), was a master at Macclesfield Grammar School in the time of Elizabeth I. He was a Latin poet and a celebrated grammarian and, as he also taught at Stratford-on-Avon, he may possibly have taught William Shakespeare. A native of Cheshire, he died at Macclesfield and there is a tablet to his memory in Macclesfield parish church.

BRUEN, John (1560–1625), was descended from the Anglo-Norman family of Le Brun. He was the squire of Stapleford and lived at the Hall. An ardent Puritan, his house became the centre for those of his persuasion and he removed the stained glass from Tarvin church and defaced the sculptured images.

BRUNNER, Sir John F. L., Bart. (1842–1919), son of a Swiss divine, was born in Liverpool. He was the co-founder of the firm of Brunner Mond of Northwich (now I.C.I.) and a noted industrialist. He was elected as the Member for Northwich in

1885 and represented this constituency until 1918.

CALDECOTT, Randolph (1846–86), was born at Chester and educated at the King's School, Chester. He became a bank clerk but his main interest was art, and his work became outstanding, his specialities being humorous illustration, and the painting of scenes of English country life including hunting.

CALVELEY, Sir Hugh (d.1393), was born at Calveley, and owned the estate of Lea. He served under Edward III in the French Wars, was made an admiral in 1378, Governor of Calais in 1377, of Brest in 1380 and later of the Channel Islands. Froissart wrote of him in his *Chronicles*. He is said to have founded a college in Rome in 1380. He appropriated the rectory of Bunbury in 1386 and founded Bunbury College for secular canons. He is buried there in a fine altar-tomb.

COTTON, Sir Stapleton (1773–1865), 1st Viscount Combermere is remembered as a brilliant soldier. He went to school in Audlem and was an M.P. from 1780–96. He fought in the Peninsular War and played a major part in the victories of Talavera and Salamanca. For five years he served as Commander in Chief in India. He was buried at Wrenbury and a monument was raised to him in Chester.

CREWE-MILNES, Robert Offley Ashburton, Marquess of Crewe (1858–1945), was born as Milnes and assumed the name Crewe-Milnes in 1894. He was descended from John Crewe of Nantwich (d.1598) who married Alice, daughter of Humphrey Mainwaring of Nantwich and both his sons were knighted. His mother married Richard Monckton Milnes, created Baron Houghton in 1863. The manor of Crewe was held by Sir Randolph Crewe in the reign of James I. The Marquess was educated at Harrow and Trinity College, Cambridge. He became Lord Houghton in 1885 and, as a prominent Liberal, held many important offices. He was made Earl of Crewe when he was Lord Lieutenant of Ireland, 1892–5. In the course of a distinguished political career he was Lord President of the Council (1905), Leader of the Government in the House of Lords (1908), Colonial Secretary (1908–10), Indian Secretary (1910–15), again Lord President (1915–16). In 1911 he was made Earl of Madeley and Marquess of Crewe. Both sons died and the title lapsed. The estate was sold to the Duchy of Lancaster in 1936, Lord Crewe dying in 1945.

DOD, John (1549?–1645), was born near Shocklach. One of Fuller's *Worthies*, he published a commentary on the Decalogue. He was educated at Jesus College, Cambridge, and became a Puritan divine.

DODGSON, Charles Lutwidge (1832–98), was better known as Lewis Carroll. Born at Daresbury vicarage, he was educated at Rugby and Christ Church, Oxford, he was ordained deacon in 1861 but did not become a priest, turning instead to writing and mathematics. He lectured in mathematics until 1881 and wrote mathematical and political books, but is chiefly remembered for *Alice in Wonderland* (1865), *Through the Looking Glass* (1871), and the *Hunting of the Snark* (1876). A memorial window in Daresbury parish church shows him with a small girl at the side of a representation of the Adoration of the Shepherds, with figures from *Alice* below.

DRAYTON, Michael (1563–1631), is linked with Cheshire, as far as is known, only by a map of 'Ches Shyre' (1612) and by the oft-quoted lines about Cheshire families in his *Polyolbion*. They refer to the battle of Bloreheath:

There Dutton, Dutton kills; a Done doth kill a
    Done;
A Booth, a Booth; and Leigh by Leigh is
    overthrown;
A Venables, against a Venables doth stand;
And Troutbeck fighteth with a Troutbeck, hand
    in hand:
There Molyneux doth make a Molyneux to die;
And Egerton the strength of Egerton doth try.

Oh, Cheshire, wert thou mad! of thine own
    native Gore,

So much until this day, thou never shed'st
   before!
Above two thousand men, upon the earth were
   thrown,
Of whom the greatest part were naturally thine
   own.

A major poet of Shakespeare's time, he is
buried in Westminster Abbey.

EGERTON, Sir Thomas (1540?–1617),
Baron Ellesmere and Viscount Brackley, was
the natural son of Sir Richard Egerton of
Ridley. Educated at Brasenose College,
Oxford, he entered Lincoln's Inn in 1559 and
was called to the bar in 1572. He became an
M.P. in 1585 while Solicitor General, and
was later Lord Chancellor of England,
Master of the Rolls, and a Privy Councillor.
A favourite of Elizabeth I, he was made
Baron Egerton in 1603 after being knighted
in 1593, and the poet Joshua Sylvester wrote
a sonnet to him. He is the ancestor of the
Egertons of Ridley and Tatton and is buried
at Dodleston church.

ELLERTON, Rev. John (1826–93), was
vicar of Crewe Green and a writer and trans-
lator of hymns. Among his best known is
'Saviour, again to Thy dear Name we raise'.

GASKELL, Mrs. Elizabeth Cleghorn (*née*
Stevenson) (1810–65), born in Chelsea, was
the daughter of a Unitarian minister and
married William Gaskell, another one. Her
mother came of a Cheshire family, the
Hollands, and Elizabeth spent most of her
childhood in Knutsford until her marriage
there. Her second book *Cranford* published in
1853 in book form is a classic picture of old
Knutsford society and is the one by which
she is best remembered, though her last book,
Wives and Daughters, is also about that town.
She is buried in the graveyard of the Unitarian chapel at Knutsford and the campanile
by the King's Coffee House is a memorial
to her.

GASTRELL, Francis, Bishop of Chester
(1662–1725) was born in Lincolnshire. He
became the Preacher of Lincoln's Inn and a
Canon of Christ Church, Oxford, and was
appointed Bishop of Chester in 1714. His

major memorial in the county is his *Notitia
Cestriensis* (published by the Chetham Society
1845–50), a remarkable record of all the
churches, schools etc. in the diocese. He was
also the means of securing the voluminous
collections of the Randle Holmes family for
posterity.

GRENFELL, Sir Wilfred (1865–1940), was
born at Mostyn House, Parkgate. He became
a medical missionary and it is for his work in
Labrador that he is remembered. There he
set up hospitals, schools, and orphanages for
the Eskimos, and is best known to this day as
'Grenfell of Labrador'.

HAMILTON, Lady Emma (1761?–1815),
was born in Ness the daughter of a poor
labourer, and baptized at Neston in 1761 as
Amy. They were so poor that her mother is
said to have hawked coal on a donkey after
being widowed. Amy Lyon went as nurse
girl first to Hawarden and then to London.
Her beauty led to her becoming the mistress
of many famous men before her marriage to
Sir William Hamilton, British Ambassador in
Naples, in 1791. She met Nelson briefly in
1793, and again in 1798, after which date she
became associated with him and bore him a
daughter in 1801. She was painted more
than twenty times by Romney as well as by
Sir Joshua Reynolds. Widowed in 1803, she
died in poverty in 1815.

HEBER, Reginald, Bishop of Calcutta (1783
–1826), was born at the Higher Rectory,
Malpas. Educated at Whitchurch Grammar
School and Brasenose College, Oxford, he
inherited the estate and the living of Hodnet
from his mother and became rector and lord
of the manor there. In 1815, he was Bampton
lecturer at Oxford and in 1822 Preacher at
Lincoln's Inn. In the same year he was offered the see of Calcutta. He was the author of
numerous religious works, poems, and hymns.
Among these last are 'From Greenland's icy
mountains' and 'Holy, holy, holy, Lord God
Almighty'. He died in Trichinopoli in 1826.

HENRY, Matthew (1662–1714), was a Non-
conformist divine and Bible commentator
who wrote the first part of his exposition of

the Old and New Testaments in Chester. Ordained in 1687, he began his ministry in that city and a meeting house was built for him in Crook Lane (now Crook Street). He was a member of the Cheshire meeting of united ministers founded at Macclesfield in 1691. He preached his last sermon from the wooden pulpit in Nantwich parish church in 1714, and died the next day after being thrown from his horse.

HIGDEN, Ranulf or Randall (d.1364), was a Benedictine monk of the community of St. Werburgh's, Chester, and a historian and playwright. His *Polychronicon*, written about 1350, was a history of the world from the Creation to his own day. He may also have been the author of the Whitsuntide plays of Chester. He is buried in the cathedral and the manuscript of the *Polychronicon* is preserved there together with a copy printed by Caxton's assistant.

HOLINSHED, Raphael (d.1580?), was born at Sutton. His *Chronicles* (1577) are the source of material for fourteen of Shakespeare's plays. They form a vast history of England, Scotland, and Ireland, beautifully written. Comparatively little is known of him except that he worked for a printer in London who died before he could complete a history of the world. His heirs reduced the plan to a history of Britain and put Holinshed in charge.

HORNBY, Albert N. (d.1925), was Captain of Lancashire Cricket, from 1880–91. He is buried in Acton churchyard with marble wickets, bails, bat, and ball over the grave.

INMAN, William (1825–81), of Upton Manor was born at Leicester and educated at the Collegiate Institute, Liverpool and Liverpool Royal Institution. He ran the first service of iron steamers between England and America in 1850 and founded the Inman Line which, by 1866, was carrying the Atlantic mails. He died at Upton Manor and was buried at Moreton parish church.

JOHNSON, Samuel, known as the 'Little Samuel Johnson' (1691–1773), was also known as 'Lord Flame'. He lived at Gawsworth and from fiddler and dancing master became a London actor and a writer of opera and plays. He is buried in a wood near Gawsworth church.

KINGSLEY, Charles (1819–75), was appointed a Canon of Chester Cathedral in 1869. From 1870–73, the writer of *The Water Babies*, lived in Chester.

LEICESTER WARREN, John Byrne, Lord de Tabley (1835–95), was born at Nether Tabley. A minor poet, a numismatologist, and a botanist, he wrote a *Flora of Cheshire*. He is buried at Lower Peover.

LEVER, W. H., 1st Viscount Leverhulme (1851–1925), was born at Bolton and began work in his father's grocery business. He travelled commercially until 1886, but in 1884 decided to launch into soap making. In 1886, he leased a soap works in Warrington. Success followed, not least because he let his workpeople join in a profit-sharing system. He used the trade name 'Sunlight' and specialized in making soap more attractive in colour, perfume, and packaging. When the Warrington site became too small, he bought land at the place which he was to name Port Sunlight. It had good railway connections, water transport by the Mersey and, from 1888 when building began, business increased rapidly. Lever Bros. became a great company with world wide connections and was later to become a series of companies linked by the name Unilever. Among his important contributions to industrial method were the fostering of good relationships with his workpeople and his building from 1889 onwards, of the garden village at Port Sunlight which ranks also as a notable social experiment.

LEYCESTER, Sir Peter (1614–78), was born at Nether Tabley and became lord of the manor. The family is said to trace its descent from the Earls of Leicester. Educated at Brasenose College, Oxford, he was imprisoned as a Royalist in Chester Castle during the Civil Wars, and created a baronet at the Restoration. He left a large collection of manuscripts, now in the possession of

Lord Tabley, and is best known as the author of *Historical Antiquities* (1673), especially the second part *Particular Remarks concerning Cheshire* which contains a valuable survey of Cheshire history and especially of Bucklow Hundred.

LUPUS, Hugh, or Hugh d'Avranches (d. 1101), known also as Hugh the Fat, was made the first Norman Earl of Chester. As such, he carried the war of conquest into North Wales and ruled Cheshire in semi-regal style. In 1092, he converted the Saxon monastery into a Benedictine abbey (now the cathedral) where he was buried in 1101. The Grosvenors (Dukes of Westminster) trace their family back to him.

MALLORY, George Leigh (d.1924), was the gallant climber who, with Andrew Irvine, was lost near the summit of Everest on the 1924 expedition. He was the son and grandson of vicars of Mobberley where he was born, and there is a memorial window to him in Mobberley church.

MARTINDALE, Adam (1623–86), was a master at Over Whitley Grammar School until 1644 when he became a Presbyterian divine. Once the incumbent of Rostherne, he left this parish after his wife cut down the maypole in protest against a pagan festival. He was befriended by Sir George Booth, 1st Viscount Delamere and served intermittently as his chaplain.

MINSHULL, Elizabeth (Mrs. John Milton) (1638–1727), was born at Wells Green Farm and baptized at Wistaston parish church in 1638. When Milton was fifty-four and already blind and with none to tend him, his doctor suggested that Elizabeth Minshull, a distant relative of Milton's, might be a suitable third wife. Elizabeth, then twenty-four, married him in Aldermanbury church, London, in 1662, and they lived at Chalfont St. Giles, Buckinghamshire, until his death in January 1678/9. She then invested the £600 which she had received under Milton's will in the lease of a farm at Brindley, near Faddiley, but her brother Richard Minshull who had done the deal for her, died in 1680, and Eliza-beth spent the rest of her life in Nantwich until her death in 1727. She is said to have been buried in the Baptist graveyard in Barker Street.

MOND, Dr. (later Sir) Robert Ludwig (1867–1938), was the son of a German scientist and became a naturalized British citizen. He was the co-founder of Brunner Mond Ltd. of Northwich and a chemist, industrialist, and archaeologist. He gave the Faraday Laboratory to the Royal Institution and made many gifts to the National Gallery.

ORMEROD, George (1785–1873), was born in Manchester, educated at King's School, Chester and at Brasenose College, Oxford. He bought an estate at Chorlton in Backford, but lived later at Sedbury Park, Gloucester-shire. In 1819, he published his monumental work *The History of the County Palatine and City of Chester* and in the same year was made a Fellow of the Royal Society. His is still the standard history of the county.

PLEGMUND, Archbishop (d.914), was a hermit of the Anglo-Saxon period who lived on what was then an island 5 miles north-east of Chester, and an eighteenth-century tomb in Plemstall is claimed as the possible site of the hermitage. Plegmund was sum-moned to the court of King Alfred, and in 890 was made Archbishop of Canterbury. He is said to have crowned Alfred's son Edward at Kingston. Plegmund's name is given to manuscript copies of the Anglo-Saxon Chronicle, and the 'Plegmund edition' is in Corpus Christi College. The Archbishop is buried at Canterbury.

PRIESTLEY, Rev. Joseph, LL.D. (1733–1804), was born near Wakefield. From 1758 to 1761, he was Unitarian minister at Nant-wich, and there is a plaque in that church in memory of him. He is remembered as a writer of books and pamphlets on education, philosophy, government, and science, but he achieved fame particularly in the last of these fields by his discovery of oxygen.

SAVAGE, Thomas (d.1507), was the second son of Sir John Savage of Clifton who built

Rock Savage, and he was born at Macclesfield. He became Archbishop of York, and intended to found a college of secular priests or canons in Macclesfield. He died at Macclesfield and was buried in York Minster, but his heart was brought back to Macclesfield and is in the Savage Chapel in Macclesfield parish church.

SHAKERLEY, Sir Geoffrey (d.1696), of Hulme Hall, Lower Peover, fought for the Royalists in the Civil Wars. He is said to have crossed the Dee in a wooden tub to get a message to King Charles during the battle of Rowton Moor. He was made Governor of Chester Castle and there is a memorial to him in Lower Peover church.

SMITH, F. E., Lord Birkenhead (1872–1930), was born at Birkenhead, the son of Frederick Smith, Barrister at law. He was educated at Birkenhead School and Wadham College, Oxford, becoming President of the Oxford Union. A brilliant debater, he had a distinguished political career. As a Conservative M.P. he held the offices of Solicitor General (1915–16), Attorney General (1916–19). In 1919 he was made Lord High Chancellor and took the title Baron Birkenhead. He held this office until 1922 and in 1924 became Secretary for India (1924–28), being created earl in 1924. He was concerned in the Irish Settlement of 1921, and in the passing of real property laws in 1922 and 1925.

SPEED, John (1552?–1629), according to Fuller's *Worthies* was born in Farndon. A tailor by trade, he became the best known of seventeenth-century cartographers, mapping the counties of England (*Atlas*, 1610), and writing *Theatre of the Empire of Great Britain* etc.

STANLEY, Arthur Penrhyn (1815–81), Dean of Westminster, was one of the Stanleys of Alderley, born at the Rectory at Alderley, second son of Edward Stanley, Bishop of Norwich. He was educated at Seaforth, Rugby, and Balliol College, Oxford, ordained deacon 1839 and priest 1843. In 1856 he was appointed to the Chair of Ecclesiastical History at Oxford and a canonry of Christ Church. This was followed in 1864 by his becoming Dean of Westminster. He published a number of works of which the best is considered to be his *Life of Arnold* (1844), and was responsible for much restoration work in Westminster Abbey.

SUTTON, Sir Richard, Kt. (d.1524), thought to have been born at Sutton near Macclesfield, was a co-founder of Brasenose College, Oxford. There is a memorial to him in Gawsworth church.

WARBURTON, Peter (1813–89), was born at Arley Hall, Northwich. He served with the East India Company for twenty years and later took official posts in Australia where he led an expedition to explore the Central Desert. His journeys are described in his book *Journey across the Western Interior of Australia* (1875). He died at Adelaide.

WILSON, Thomas, (1663–1755), was born at Burton in Wirral and educated at King's School, Chester and Trinity College, Dublin. In 1697 he became Bishop of Sodor and Man and the degree of Doctor of Laws was conferred in the following year. Generous and self-sacrificing, he called himself the poorest bishop in Europe, but Dean Farrar said he was 'the last survivor of the saints in the English church'. He was Bishop in the Island for fifty-eight years.

BIBLIOGRAPHY

Allison, J. E., *The Mersey Estuary*, Liverpool, 1949.

Bagshaw, S., *History, Gazetteer and Directory of the County Palatine of Chester*, Sheffield, 1850.

Barker, T. C., 'Lancashire Coal, Cheshire Salt, and the Rise of Liverpool', *Trans. Hist. Soc. Lancs. and Ches.*, *CII*, 1950.

Barraclough, Geoffrey, 'The Earldom and County Palatine of Chester', *Trans. Hist. Soc. Lancs. and Ches.*, *CIII*, 1951.

Beck, Joan, *Tudor Cheshire*, Chester, 1969.

Boon, E. P., *Cheshire*, Land Utilization Survey Report, London, 1941.

Brownbill, John, *West Kirby and Hilbre, a parochial history*, Liverpool, 1928.

Burne, R. V. H., *The Monks of Chester*, S.P.C.K., London, 1962.

Calvert, A. F., *Salt in Cheshire*, London and New York, 1915.

Chaloner, W. H., *The Social and Economic History of Crewe 1780–1923*, Manchester, 1950.

Chapman, W. Dobson, *County Palatine: A Plan for Cheshire*, Chester, 1948.

Crossley, F. H., *Cheshire*, London, 1949.

Crump, W. B., 'Saltways from the Cheshire Wiches', *Trans. Lancs. and Ches. Ant. Soc.*, *LIV*, 1939.

Davies, C. Stella, *The Agricultural History of Cheshire 1750–1850*, Chetham Society, Manchester, 1960.

Davies, C. Stella, *A History of Macclesfield*, Manchester, 1961.

Dore, R. N., *The Civil Wars in Cheshire*, Chester, 1966.

Earwaker, J. P., *East Cheshire*, 2 vols., London, 1887–8.

Forde-Johnston, J., 'The Iron Age Hill Forts of Lancashire and Cheshire', *Trans. Lancs. and Ches. Ant. Soc.*, *LXXII*, 1962.

Green, Henry, *Knutsford, its Traditions and History*, 2nd ed., Manchester, 1887.

Greville, M. D., 'Chronological List of the Railways of Cheshire', *Trans. Hist. Soc. Lancs. and Ches.*, *CV*, 1954.

Hadfield, *British Canals*, London, 1950.

Hall, James, *A History of the Town and Parish of Nantwich*, Nantwich, 1883.

Harrison, W., 'The Development of the Turnpike System in Lancashire and Cheshire', *Trans. Lancs. Ant. Soc.*, *IV*, 1886.

Harrison, W., 'Pre-Turnpike Highways in Lancashire and Cheshire', *Trans. Lancs. and Ches. Ant. Soc.*, *IX*, 1891.

Heginbotham, Henry, *Stockport, Ancient and Modern*, 2 vols., London, 1882–92.

Hewitt, J., *Medieval Cheshire*, Chetham Soc., Manchester, 1929.

Hewitt, J., *Cheshire under the Three Edwards*, Chester, 1967.

Holland, H., *General View of the Agriculture of Cheshire*, London, 1808.

King, Daniel, *Vale Royal of England*, London, 1656.

Leycester, Sir Peter, *Historical Antiquities, Book II, Particular Remarks concerning Cheshire*, London, 1673.

Lysons, D. and S., *Magna Britannia, Vol. II, Pt. II, The County Palatine of Chester*, London, 1810.

Marker, Margaret E., 'The Dee Estuary: its progressive silting and salt marsh development', *Trans. Inst. Brit. Geographers*, *41*, 1967.

Mee, Arthur, ed. *Cheshire*, King's England Series, London, 1938.

Morris, R. H., *Chester in the Plantagenet and Tudor Reigns*, Chester, 1894.

Norris, J. Harold, 'The Water-powered Corn Mills of Cheshire', *Trans. Lancs. and Ches. Ant. Soc.*, *LXXV–LXXVI*, 1965–6.

Ormerod, George, *The History of the County Palatine and City of Chester*, 3 vols., 2nd ed. edited by Thos. Helsby, London, 1882.

Potter, Simeon, 'Cheshire Place-names', *Trans. Hist. Soc. Lancs. and Ches., CVI,* 1954.

Priestley, Joseph, *Historical Account of the Navigable Rivers, Canals, and Railways through Great Britain,* London, 1831.

Reilly, Sir Chas. and N. J. Aslan, *Outline Plan for the County Borough of Birkenhead,* Birkenhead, 1947.

Richards, Raymond, *Old Cheshire Churches,* London, 1947.

Rideout, E. H., *The Growth of Wirral,* Liverpool, 1927.

Singleton, W. A., 'Traditional House-Types in Lancashire and Cheshire', *Trans. Hist. Soc. Lancs. and Ches., CIV,* 1952.

Smith, Wilfred, ed. *Merseyside, A Scientific Survey,* Brit. Assocn., 1953.

Stephens, W. B. ed. *History of Congleton,* Manchester, 1970.

Stephens, W. B. 'The Overseas Trade of Chester in the Early Seventeenth Century', *Trans. Hist. Soc. Lancs. and Ches., CXX,* 1968.

Sylvester, Dorothy and Geoffrey Nulty, ed. *The Historical Atlas of Cheshire,* Chester, 1958.

Sylvester, Dorothy and H. B. Rodgers, *Crewe: A Geographic, Economic and Demographic Study of the Town in relation to S. E. Cheshire,* Report for the Borough Council of Crewe, 1965.

Sylvester, Dorothy, 'The Open Fields of Cheshire', *Trans. Hist. Soc. Lancs. and Ches., CVIII,* 1956.

Sylvester, Dorothy, 'The Manor and the Cheshire Landscape', *Trans. Lancs. and Ches. Ant. Soc., LXX,* 1960.

Sylvester, Dorothy, 'Cheshire in the Dark Ages', *Trans. Hist. Soc. Lancs. and Ches., CXIV,* 1962.

Sylvester, Dorothy, 'Parish and Township in Cheshire and N.E. Wales', *Journ. Chester Archaeol. Soc., LIV,* 1967.

Tait, James, ed. *The Domesday Survey of Cheshire,* Chetham Soc., 1916.

Thompson, F. H., *Deva, Roman Chester,* Chester, 1959.

Thompson, F. H., *Roman Cheshire,* Chester, 1965.

Varley, W. J. and J. W. Jackson, with maps by Lily F. Chitty, *Prehistoric Cheshire,* Chester, 1940.

Varley, W. J., *Cheshire before the Romans,* Chester, 1964.

Wainwright, F. T., 'North-west Mercia, A.D. 871–924', *Trans. Hist. Soc. Lancs. and Ches., XCIV,* 1942.

Wallis, P. J., 'A Preliminary Register of Old Schools in Lancashire and Cheshire', *Trans. Hist. Soc. Lancs. and Ches., CXX,* 1968.

Wallwork, K. L., 'Subsidence in the Mid-Cheshire Industrial Area', *Geog. Journ., CXXII,* 1956.

Watkins, W. T., *Roman Cheshire,* Liverpool, 1886.

Wedge, Thos., *General View of the Agriculture of Cheshire,* London, 1794.

White, Francis and Co., *Gazetteer and Directory of Cheshire,* Sheffield, 1860.

Willan, T. S., *The Navigation of the River Weaver in the Eighteenth Century,* Chetham Society, Manchester, 1951.

A CHRONOLOGICAL TABLE

circa 8000 B.C.   First northern movement of Man in Britain
circa 8000–5000 B.C.   Mesolithic occupation
circa 3000 B.C.   Men of Neolithic culture reached Cheshire area
circa 1750–1550 B.C.   Bronze Age in this area
circa mid-sixth century B.C.   Early Iron Age began in Cheshire
55 & 54 B.C.   Julius Caesar attempted to conquer Britain

43   Successful Claudian invasion of Britain
60 or 61   Suetonius Paulinus invaded Anglesey, probably from Chester
79   Chester manned by the Second Legion
circa 86–7   Chester garrisoned by the Twentieth Legion
410   Final withdrawal of the Romans from Britain
600–50   Anglo-Saxon occupation of the Welsh Borderland including Cheshire
870–924   Irish-Norse incursions into, and settlement of, Wirral
913–19   The Lady Ethelfleda fortified Cheshire against the Danes
980   Second Danish raid into Cheshire
1069–70   William the Conqueror's mid-winter march into Cheshire from Yorkshire
1071   Hugh d'Avranches (or Hugh Lupus) created 1st Norman Earl of Chester
1086   Domesday Book compiled
1215–16   *Carta Communis Cestriensis*—'The Magna Carta of Cheshire'—drawn up
1237   The last Norman Earl of Chester died and the earldom passed to the Crown
1284   By the terms of the Treaty of Rhuddlan Flintshire became a county, 'shired' from Cheshire
1349   The Black Death
1485   Accession of the Tudors. The 'end of the Middle Ages'
1536   The first of the Welsh Acts which dealt with the Union of England and Wales. Denbighshire now became a county
1555   The Highway Act. Road maintenance became the responsibility of the parish
1637   The first public coach plied between Birmingham and Holyhead via Nantwich and Chester
1663   The first Turnpike Trust formed. Magistrates and surveyors made responsible for road maintenance
1670   Rock salt discovered near Northwich
1700   Brine springs discovered near Winsford
1720   Acts passed for the construction of parts of the Weaver Navigation and the Mersey and Irwell Navigation
1732   Weaver Navigation opened to traffic
A Stockport silk mill set up using water-powered machinery
1754   The New Cut straightened the sea approach to Chester
1759   Bridgewater Canal Act
1767   Bridgewater Canal extended to Runcorn
1779   Crompton's Mule invented

1780   First Mail Coach reached Holyhead via Nantwich and Chester
         Great Marston salt mine opened to exploit the lower salt bed
1785   Cartwright's power loom
1805   Union of Great Britain and Ireland, enhancing importance of Holyhead route
1815–30   Holyhead road re-routed via Shrewsbury and Llangollen
1817   First steam ferry boat plied on the River Mersey between Tranmere and Liverpool
1824   William Laird built iron works near Wallasey Pool
1828   The first ships built at Birkenhead
1837   The first railway on Cheshire soil, the Grand Junction, linked Birmingham and Warrington
1843   Grand Junction railway works opened in Monks Coppenhall
         Growth of Crewe town began
1847   First chemical works opened at Widnes
1874   Brunner Mond works opened at Winnington
1888   Cheshire County Council formed under the Local Government Act
1888–9   William Lever's soap factory built and Port Sunlight founded
1902   Ellesmere Port became an Urban District and major growth began
1926   Link-up of National Electricity Grid in progress
1934   First Mersey road tunnel opened between Liverpool and Birkenhead
1937   Ministry of Transport became responsible for the upkeep of main and trunk roads
1947   Congleton designated a New Town
1961   Electrification completed of the Crewe–Manchester and the Crewe–Liverpool railway lines
         Runcorn road bridge opened
1962   New Queensferry road bridge opened
1963   Cheshire portion of the M6 opened
1964   Runcorn designated a New Town

INDEX